CROCHET
FOR BEGINNERS

LEARN TO CROCHET WITH 19 HOT PROJECTS

SUSIE JOHNS

CARROLL & BROWN PUBLISHERS LIMITED

First published in 2004 in the United Kingdom by

Carroll & Brown Publishers Limited
20 Lonsdale Road
London NW6 6RD

Project Editor Caroline Smith
Managing Art Editor Emily Cook
Photographer Jules Selmes

Patterns copyright © Susie Johns 2004
Illustrations and compilation © Carroll & Brown Limited 2004

A CIP catalogue record for this book is available from the British Library.

ISBN: 978-1-903258-92-7

1098765432

Reproduced by RDC, Malaysia
Printed in China

CONTENTS

INTRODUCTION

Ready, set, crochet! One of the most versatile of handicrafts, crochet is easy to learn, simple to do, and requires very little in the way of materials – just a hook and a ball of yarn.

Crochet's charm lies in its simplicity: there are very few basic stitches to learn but they can be combined to create an almost infinite variety of patterns and textures. Used imaginatively, crochet can create a fabric that is firm and hard-edged, one that is soft and flexible, one that is intricate and detailed, or one that is light, open, and delicate. Crochet can be worked in rows or in the round, to form not only flat fabrics but shaped and contoured ones, too. Many crocheted items can be worked in one piece – so there's no sewing up and no bulky seams.

Crochet is also quick! Most of the patterns in this book could be completed in a few sessions. Buy the hook and yarn today and you could be wearing your own hand-made hat, scarf or bikini top in a matter of days.

This book starts you off with a few fundamentals: the basic stitches, the best working practices, and the techniques you'll need to shape your crochet. Two quick and simple patterns follow: a pretty bikini top and a fabulous funky belt, both of which you can easily make in a couple of evenings.

By manipulating those basic stitches, you can give your crochet new texture and interest. Using different coloured yarns will also add a new element to your crochet. You'll find information here on changing colours and using graphs, followed by a pattern for a stylish striped top. More variations on the basic techniques follow, along with patterns that put the methods you have learned into practice.

Crochet pieces are often worked in the round. You'll find a simple explanation of the basic technique and how it is adapted to create some stunning shapes as well as practical clothes and bags. A section on raised patterns follows, showing you just how versatile crochet can be as you create cables, bobbles and bullion stitches.

Part of crochet's traditional appeal lies in the lacy, open look that can be achieved. Here, you'll find information on how to create this kind of work, from simple picot edgings to delicate filet crochet. As with all the techniques described in this book, you'll find plenty of patterns that give you the chance to use your new found skills. Patterns that, hopefully, will inspire you to take up this exciting, but age-old, handicraft.

Although crochet is a traditional craft, it certainly isn't stuck in the past. Every year new designers discover its unique appeal. New stitch patterns are invented, new garments are produced, and another generation is encouraged to learn the simple skills required for this creative craft.

You'll also find that there's an inspiring range of different yarns available to use in your work – from traditional crochet cottons to multi-hued novelty yarns. And you don't have to stop there. Try using string. Dye your own yarn. Try leather lacing, ribbons, or strips of fabric, either cut or torn. Add beads, buttons or appliqué, and combine crochet with knitting. The possibilities, as the saying goes, are limited only by your imagination.

As more and more people appreciate hand-made textiles and the value of traditional crafts, crochet, now more than ever, has so much to offer. I hope this book gets you hooked!

HOOKS AND YARNS

HOOKS AND YARNS

Crochet hooks come in different sizes and materials. There are fine steel hooks and larger ones made of aluminum, plastic, or wood. Yarns are sold by weight and/or length. Beginners will find it helpful to choose a smooth yarn in a heavy weight that is not likely to untwist while you work. Generally, the coarser the yarn, the larger the hook you will need.

HOOKS

Crochet hooks are labelled in several ways – a letter, number, and/or a metric measurement. Steel and aluminum hooks come in a large range of sizes, but wooden hooks are also popular. Avoid cheaper plastic versions that may have rough edges. Tunisian crochet needs a very long hook (shown at the bottom here) that has either a knob at the end, similar to that on a knitting needle, or another hook.

Sometimes a hook size is given on the yarn's label: use this as a starting point to obtain the correct tension (see pages 18–19). Novelty yarns can be worked with a larger hook than a smooth yarn of similar weight. If you are mixing more than one yarn in a garment, check that they share the same care instructions.

CROCHET HOOK SIZES

Metric sizes		US sizes
2mm	=	Size B
2.25mm	=	Size 1
2.5mm	=	Size C
2.75mm	=	Size 2
3mm	=	Size D
3.25mm	=	Size 3
3.5mm	=	Size E
3.5mm	=	Size 4
3.75mm	=	Size 5
4mm	=	Size F
4.25mm	=	Size 6
4.5mm	=	Size G
4.5mm	=	Size 7
5mm	=	Size H
5mm	=	Size 8
5.5mm	=	Size I
5.5mm	=	Size 9
6mm	=	Size J
6mm	=	Size 10
6.5mm	=	Size 10½
7mm	=	Size K
8mm	=	Size 11
9mm	=	Size 13
10mm	=	Size 15
Steel hooks		
2.5mm	=	Size 0
2mm	=	Size 1
1.75mm	=	Size 4
1.5mm	=	Size 6
1mm	=	Size 10
0.75mm	=	Size 12

YARNS

There are standard terms for the most popular weights of yarns. These yarns may be made of different numbers of strands spun together, 2-, 3- and 4-ply are all common. Fine weight or 2-ply is usually used for lace work and edgings. It is approximately half the thickness of 3-ply, or finer; 3-ply is used for delicate garments and baby items. Four-ply, middle of the weight range, is for sweaters, cardigans or shawls, and is the standard on which other yarn weights are based. Double knitting is for chunkier jackets and sweaters, and is equivalent to two strands of 4-ply. Aran weight is equivalent to three strands of 4-ply, and is used for heavy afghans or jackets. Chunky, for warm outdoor garments, is equivalent to four strands of 4-ply or two strands of double knitting.

BEGINNING TO CROCHET

Crochet work, like knitting, is created from a continuous length of yarn.

In crochet a single hook is used to work one stitch at a time.

You start with a slip knot then continue to make loops (called chains) to

form a foundation chain from which you make the first row.

LEFT-HANDED CROCHETERS

If you are left-handed, hold the working yarn in your right hand and hold the hook in the left hand.

Before you get started, it's a good idea to become comfortable with holding the hook and yarn. You can hold them any way you like, as long as you can work freely and your hands don't feel cramped. Here, we show the two most common ways of holding the hook but you could devise a method to suit yourself.

The two most common methods of controlling yarn are also shown here. The way you hold yarn does have an important part to play – the yarn tension is controlled with your middle finger or forefinger. As you crochet, you want to be able to control the yarn evenly and work uniform chains, so practice the different methods to find which one is easiest for you.

HOLDING THE HOOK

Both methods are equally good, so use whichever feels most comfortable.

Pencil position
Grasp the flat part of the hook between thumb and forefinger as if it were a pencil with the stem above your hand.

Knife position
With the stem against your palm and your thumb on the flat part, grasp the hook between thumb and fingers.

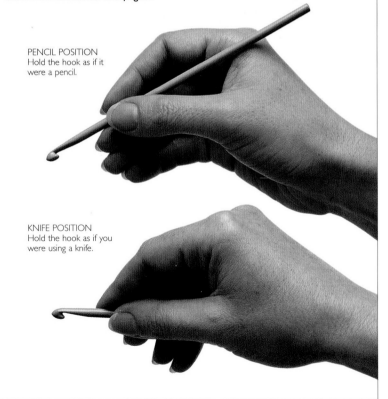

PENCIL POSITION
Hold the hook as if it were a pencil.

KNIFE POSITION
Hold the hook as if you were using a knife.

MAKING A SLIP KNOT

To begin crochet you need to make a slip knot. About 15cm (6in) from the yarn end, make a loop. Insert the hook and catch the working yarn, drawing it up through the loop. Pull both ends to tighten the knot and then slide it up to the hook.

CONTROLLING THE YARN

The way you hold the yarn allows it to flow easily with the right tension. You can wrap the yarn around your little finger, over the next two fingers, and catch it with your forefinger – when your middle finger will control the yarn. Or you can wrap the yarn around your little finger, then under your next two fingers and over your forefinger – when your forefinger will control the yarn. With thick yarn, you can catch it between your fourth and fifth fingers. Use the method that feels most comfortable.

FOREFINGER METHOD

Pass the working yarn around the little finger, under the next two fingers and over the forefinger (*top*). With the hook through the slip loop, and holding the slip knot between thumb and middle finger of the left hand, prepare to make the first chain by raising your forefinger.

MIDDLE FINGER METHOD

Pass the working yarn around the little finger, and over the other fingers (*right*). With the hook through the slip loop, and holding the slip knot between the thumb and forefinger of the left hand, prepare to make the first chain by raising your middle finger.

FOUNDATION STITCHES

The first row of a piece of crochet is called the foundation chain. It may be short – just one or two stitches – or it may be quite long. This chain is the base for the remaining work and needs to be neat and even.

COUNTING CHAINS

Each chain (loop) counts as one stitch. To count the chains correctly, make sure that they are not twisted and that the fronts are facing you. The loop currently on the hook is never counted as a stitch, nor is the slip knot at the beginning of the foundation chain. There is always one loop left on the hook after completing every stitch, and this is referred to as the working loop.

Once you've made yourself comfortable with your hook and yarn and formed your first slip knot (see pages 8–9), you are ready to make a foundation chain. Chain stitch (abbreviated to *ch*) is usually used. This is simply made by pulling the yarn through the slip knot and then each subsequent loop on the hook. Chain stitch is also used as part of a pattern stitch, to make spaces between stitches, for bars in openwork (see page 77), and for the turning chains at the beginnings of rows/rounds (see pages 16 and 53). The length of the foundation chain will be specified in the pattern instruction.

Slip stitch (abbreviated to *sl st*) is the most basic of crochet stitches – some of the earliest crochet work found was done in continuous slip stitch – and is made by simply drawing the yarn through the work and the loop on the hook at the same time. Today, slip stitch is used most commonly to join a row into a round (see page 53), to decrease (see page 22), and for joining seams (see pages 26–27), although you will find it used occasionally for a variety of patterns.

Your work begins with a good foundation chain – and further chains can be put to good use to make simple cords and ties (see pages 58–59).

FOUNDATION CHAIN

The foundation chain should be worked loosely and evenly to ensure that the hook can enter each loop easily on the first row. The hook and your tension will determine the size of the chains. Do not try to make chains loose by pulling them as you make them, since this tightens up previously made chains. If the chains are too tight, ensure that the yarn is flowing through your fingers easily, or use a larger hook than you will use for the rest of your work. The number of chains for the foundation chain will be specified in the pattern instruction.

MAKING A CHAIN STITCH (ch)

1 Hold the hook in your right hand. Keeping the working yarn taut, grasp the slip knot with the thumb and middle finger of your left hand. Push the hook forward and take the hook under (anti-clockwise), behind and then over the yarn, so that the yarn passes round the hook and is caught in it. This is called yarn round hook – or yrh.

2 Draw the hook and yarn back through the slip loop to form the first chain stitch.

3 Repeat steps 1 and 2. After making a few chains in this way, move your left hand up so that you are holding the work directly under the hook for maximum control, and continue.

MAKING A SLIP STITCH (sl st)

1 Make a length of evenly worked foundation chain.

2 Insert the hook from front to back under the top of the second chain (ch) from the hook. Wrap the yarn around the hook (yrh).

3 Draw the yarn through the two loops now on the hook, making a slip stitch. To continue working slip stitch, insert the hook into the next and each chain, and repeat step 2 as required.

BASIC STITCHES

It is easy to learn crochet stitches because they are all made the same way.

Apart from the chain and the slip stitch, there are five basic crochet stitches,

which vary in height (there are others, but these tend to be more advanced

and are used less frequently).

The difference in the height or length of these stitches is determined by the number of times the yarn is wrapped around the hook. As each stitch has a flatter appearance on the front than on the back, the crocheted piece has more texture when worked in rows and turned because you see both the fronts and the backs of the stitches. The surface has a smoother, flatter look when worked in rows/rounds without turning, as it always shows the front of the stitches.

✤ TREBLE CROCHET (tr) (see page 15)
Twice as high as double crochet, this stitch works up quickly and is one of the most popular stitches

✤ HALF TREBLE CROCHET (htr)
Between double and treble crochet in size, this stitch produces a slightly looser surface with an attractive ridge.

✤ DOUBLE CROCHET (dc)
This simple compact stitch (left) is found in many pattern designs and forms a firm, smooth surface.

DOUBLE CROCHET (dc)

1 *Make a foundation chain. Skip 2 ch and insert the hook under top loop of 3rd ch.*

2 *Yrh and draw yarn through the chain loop only.*

3 *There are 2 loops on the hook. Yrh and draw the yarn through both loops. Double crochet (dc) made.*

4 *Continue working dc into the next and all following chains to the end of the row.*

5 *To make next and following rows of dc, turn work and ch 1. This is the turning chain (t-ch) and counts as first dc in new row. Skip the first st, at base of t-ch, work 1 dc into top 2 loops of 2nd st in previous row. Work 1 dc into next and each st to end, including top of t-ch.*

HALF TREBLE CROCHET (htr)

1 *Make a foundation chain. Skip 2 ch, yrh and insert the hook under top loop of 3rd ch, yrh.*

2 *Draw the yarn through the chain loop only (there are 3 loops on hook), yrh.*

3 *Draw the yarn through all 3 loops. Half treble crochet (htr) made. Continue working htr into next and all following chs to end of the row.*

4 *To make next and following rows of htr, turn work and ch 2. This is the t-ch and counts as first htr in new row. Skip the first st at base of t-ch, work 1 htr into top 2 loops of 2nd st in previous row. Work 1 htr into next and each st to end, including top of t-ch.*

MORE BASIC STITCHES

MORE BASIC STITCHES

Whenever you are working the basic stitches, shown here and on page 12, onto the foundation chain, insert the hook from front to back under the top loop of each chain. On subsequent rows, unless instructed otherwise, insert your hook from front to back under the top two loops of each stitch.

At the end of each row, turn the work then make extra chains, called turning chains, to bring the hook level with the height of the stitches in the new row (see pages 16–17). The turning chains may or may not count as stitches at the beginning of a row, according to the pattern. They do count as stitches in the basic stitch patterns shown on pages 13 and 15.

❖ TRIPLE TREBLE CROCHET (ttr)

This extremely long stitch is used in fancy stitch patterns, but is not generally used continuously to make a whole piece, except where it is linked (see page 33).

❖ DOUBLE TREBLE CROCHET (dtr)

Three times as high as double crochet, this stitch (left) forms an open, looser texture.

TREBLE CROCHET (tr)

1 *Make a foundation chain. Skip 3 ch, yrh and insert the hook under the top loop of 4th ch, yrh.*

2 *Draw the yarn through the ch loop only (there are 3 loops on the hook), yrh.*

3 *Draw the yarn through 2 loops only (2 loops on hook), yrh.*

4 *Draw the yarn through these 2 loops. Treble crochet (tr) made. Continue working tr into next and all following chains to end of the row. To make next and following rows of tr, turn work and ch 3. This is the t-ch and counts as first tr in new row. Skip the first st at base of t-ch, work 1 tr into top 2 loops of 2nd st in previous row. Work 1 tr into next and each st to end, including into top of t-ch.*

DOUBLE TREBLE (dtr)

1 *Make a foundation chain. Skip 4 ch, yrh twice, insert hook under top loop of 5th ch. Yrh, draw yarn through ch loop only (4 loops on hook), yrh.*

2 *Draw yarn through 2 loops only (3 loops on hook), yrh. Draw yarn through 2 loops only, yrh. Draw yarn through remaining 2 loops; double treble (dtr) made. Dtr into next and following chs. To make next row of dtr, turn work and ch 4. This t-ch counts as first tr in new row. Skip first st at base of t-ch. Work 1 dtr, inserting hook under top 2 loops of 2nd st in previous row; continue.*

TRIPLE TREBLE (ttr)

1 *Make a foundation chain. Skip 5 chs, yrh 3 times and insert hook under top loop of 6th ch. Yrh, draw yarn through ch loop only (5 loops on the hook), *Yrh, draw yarn through 2 loops only.*

2 *Repeat from * three times more; triple treble (ttr) made. Ttr into next and following chs. To make the next row, turn work and ch 5. This t-ch counts as first ttr in new row. Skip first st at base of t-ch. Work 1 ttr, inserting hook under top 2 loops of the 2nd st in previous row; continue.*

WORKING PRACTICE

WORKING PRACTICE

In crochet, there are some basic techniques to master and useful practices to follow that will help you as you work. Keep these methods in mind as you crochet and you'll get a neater finish.

TURNING CHAINS (t-ch)

To bring the hook up to the height of the stitches, you must add turning chains at the beginning of each row. Each of the basic stitches (see pages 12–15) has its own number of chains: the table below gives the numbers when the t-ch counts as the first stitch. Sometimes the t-ch may not be counted as a stitch (see Straight Edges, page 17). Some instructions say ch 2 and turn.

STITCH	Add to foundation chain	Skip at beginning of foundation row (counts as first st)	For turning chain counts as first st
Double	1	2	1
Half treble	1	2	2
Treble	2	3	3
Double treble	3	4	4
Triple treble	4	5	5

COUNTING STITCHES

To count short stitches, such as double crochet (as shown), it is easier to look at the tops. For longer stitches, count the upright stems – each is counted as a single stitch.

5 4 3 2 1

FASTENING OFF

To prevent the work from unravelling when you have finished, it is necessary to fasten the end. Complete the final stitch, then cut the working yarn and pull it through the last loop on the hook. Pull the yarn tight to close the loop. Thread the working end of the yarn into a tapestry or yarn needle and weave it into the back of the work.

WORKING IN ROWS

Crochet is normally worked in rows to produce the desired width, and the work is turned between each row. The right side of the work will not always be facing you.

1 *The first row is made by working across the foundation chain from right to left (if you are left-handed, work from left to right).*

2 *At the end of the foundation chain or row, turn the work so that the yarn is behind the hook and the new stitches can be worked into the tops of those in the previous row.*

STRAIGHT EDGES

To obtain straight edges and keep the number of stitches constant, you need to make the turning chains in one of two ways. The first is the most common, but the second is used with very short stitches, or to avoid the gap created by using the turning chain as a stitch. However, the second method creates slightly uneven edges.

TURNING CHAIN COUNTS AS FIRST STITCH

Skip the first stitch of the previous row at the base of the t-ch (right). When you reach the end of the row (far right), work a stitch into the top of the t-ch of the previous row.

TURNING CHAIN DOES NOT COUNT AS STITCH

Work into the first stitch at the base of the t-ch (right). When you reach the end of the row (far right), do not work into the top of the previous t-ch.

TENSION

TENSION

The number of stitches and rows that are required to make a piece of crochet of a specific size depends upon four things: the yarn, the hook size, the stitch pattern and the individual crocheter.

At the beginning of every crochet pattern you will find the tension. This indicates the number of stitches and rows in a particular measure, i.e. 15dc = 10cm (4in) (15 double crochets = 10cm (4in)) – and the entire design is based around this. To achieve the best results, you must follow the tension. But since crochet is a true handcraft, each person's work will be slightly different. Before beginning a project, make a swatch to ensure that your tension matches that given. If you want to change the yarn or the stitch pattern, you can usually do so as long as you can still match the tension.

MAKING ADJUSTMENTS

If, after making your sample, your tension does not correspond with that given in the instructions, change to a bigger or smaller hook and crochet another sample.

Fewer stitches and rows than indicated means your work is too loose and you should try a smaller hook. More stitches and rows than shown means it is too tight and you should try a larger hook.

Occasionally you may find it impossible to match the tension of both stitches and rows at the same time, in which case you should match the stitch tension and compensate by working more or fewer rows, as necessary.

CHECKING THE TENSION

Using the weight of yarn, hook size and stitch pattern given with the instructions, crochet a sample at least 10cm (4in) square. Place the finished sample right side up on a flat surface, taking care not to stretch it out of shape.

MEASURING STITCHES

Lay your ruler across the sample at the bottom of a row of stitches. Insert two pins vertically 10cm (4in) apart. Count the number of stitches between the pins.

MEASURING ROWS

Now turn your ruler vertically and lay it along one side of a column of stitches. Avoiding the edges, place pins horizontally 10cm (4in) apart. Count the rows between the pins.

THE EFFECT OF YARNS AND PATTERNS

The weight of the yarn that you are using and the stitch pattern affect the tension, so always work a sample before altering written instructions. Fine yarn will work with more stitches to the measure than a heavier yarn, as will yarn worked with a smaller hook.

DIFFERENT YARNS

A thick yarn and a finer yarn worked on the same hook size and same stitch will result in different numbers of stitches over the measure.

DIFFERENT HOOK SIZES

The same yarn and stitch worked on different size hooks will work up to a different tension.

DIFFERENT STITCHES

Different stitch patterns worked with the same hook and the same yarn will also produce different numbers of stitches over the measure.

INCREASING

Many crocheted items are made of simple squares or rectangles worked evenly throughout to create a flat piece of work. There are times, however, when it is necessary to shape your work by making it wider. This can be done by increasing, that is by adding stitches.

There are many reasons why you might want to add stitches to your crochet work. If you are making a garment, you will want to fit it to the shape of the body. Adding stitches at the right place will make your work wider exactly where it is needed.

Increasing while working in the round helps add new elements to the pattern at the same time as changing the shape of whatever you are making. In fact, increases can be used to create many decorative crochet patterns.

The easiest way to increase is to work twice into one stitch (a single increase). You can do this at the beginning and end of rows, to shape the work at the sides, or across a row. If you need to add more than two stitches, to make multiple increases, you can do this at the beginning and end of rows by working additional chain stitches. This won't give you a gradual shaping, the increase will form a definite angle at the edge of the work.

As you work this pretty summer hat, you increase the stitches to help shape the crown (see page 56) .

WORKING SINGLE INCREASES

When it is necessary to increase by a single stitch, the simplest way is to work twice into the same stitch. When you are making single increases one above another, across a row, work each subsequent pair into either the first or second of the previous pair consistently, so as to maintain lines of increase. To slant them to the right on a right side row, work each increase pair into the first of the previous pair; to slant them to the left, work them into the second.

AT THE BEGINNING OF A ROW

When the turning chain counts as a stitch (see pages 16–17): skip the first st as usual and work 2 sts into the 2nd st, or work 1 st into the first st that you usually skip.

AT THE END OF A ROW

Work 2 sts into the last st (this will be the turning chain, if it counts as a st).

ACROSS A ROW

Pattern instructions usually tell you where to position each increase, but if not, spread them evenly across the row. Work 2 sts into the one below at each position.

MULTIPLE INCREASES

To increase by more than two stitches at the edge, make additional chain stitches. The method is the same for all the basic stitches. Here the turning chain counts as a stitch. When several stitches at once are made at an edge, a sharp angle is created.

AT THE BEGINNING OF A ROW

Add the the number of increases needed to the number of turning chains being used. For example, if you are working treble crochet (tr), which needs 2 t-ch, and want to add 3 sts, you will need to work 5 ch (left). Skip 3 ch (counts as 1 tr) and work 1 tr into each of the remaining 2 new chs, making 3 new sts, including t-ch (right).

AT THE END OF A ROW

To make the first additional increase stitch, insert the hook through the lower part of the last stitch made, picking up the single, vertical thread on its left-hand side (left). Continue inserting the hook into the base of the stitch just completed to work the required number of additional stitches (right).

DECREASING

By decreasing, you can give crocheted garments form and create openings, such as necklines and armholes.

It may be necessary to shape your crochet work by subtracting stitches. These decreases may be made at the beginning and/or end of a row, or at set places within the row. You also can narrow your work by skipping one or more stitches, but this method can leave holes. Unless you want the decorative effect created by holes, it is preferable to decrease by the method shown here (see right) or by crocheting two or more stitches together, in a stitch cluster (see page 23).

When working single decrease clusters one above another, in mid row, work consistently either the first or second part of the cluster into the top of the previous cluster to maintain the lines of decrease.

Decreasing plays an important role in shaping a garment to fit (see page 40).

MULTIPLE DECREASES

You can decrease by more than one stitch at the ends of rows by omitting stitches. At the beginning of rows, you slip stitch over the number of stitches you want to decrease and at the ends you simply leave stitches unworked. This method creates a sharp angle. To create a more gradual decrease, work stitches together in a cluster (see page 23). Treble crochet (tr) is shown here, but the method is the same for all basic stitches. The turning chain counts as a stitch.

AT THE BEGINNING OF A ROW

Work slip st over each stitch to be subtracted. Then make the required turning chain to form a new edge st.itch Continue the row in pattern.

AT THE END OF A ROW

Work in pattern until you reach the stitches to be decreased. Leave these stitches unworked, turn and make the turning chain for the first stitch of the next row.

WORKING A STITCH CLUSTER

To decrease one, two, three, etc. stitches, work two, three, four, etc. stitches together. At the beginning of a row, when the turning chain counts as the first stitch, work the second and third stitches together to make a single decrease and the second, third, and fourth together to make a double decrease. At the end of a row, work the last two, three, or four stitches together. In mid row, work one, two, or three consecutive stitches together in the appropriate positions. The steps here describe single and double decreases at the beginning of rows for double, half treble, and treble crochet. The method is the same for longer crochet stitches, such as double treble crochet.

DOUBLE CROCHET (dc)

Single decrease: Ch 1 (counts as 1 dc), skip first st, *insert hook into 2nd st, yrh and draw through**; rep from *once more into 3rd st (3 loops on hook), ending yrh and draw through all loops – single decrease (dc2tog) made.

Double decrease: Work as for single decrease from *, but rep from * to ** once more into 4th st (4 loops on hook) before ending. Double decrease (dc3tog) made.

HALF TREBLE CROCHET (htr)

Single decrease: Ch 2 (counts as 1 htr), skip first st, *yrh, insert hook into 2nd st, yrh and draw through**; rep from * once more into 3rd st (5 loops on hook), ending yrh and draw through all loops – single decrease (htr2tog) made.

Double decrease: Work as for single decrease from *, but rep from * to ** once more into 4th st (7 loops on hook) before ending. Double decrease (htr3tog) made.

TREBLE CROCHET (tr)

Single decrease: Ch 3 (counts as 1 tr), skip first st, *yrh, insert hook into 2nd st, yrh and draw through, yrh and draw through 2 loops only**; rep from * once more into 3rd st (3 loops on hook), ending yrh and draw through all loops— single decrease (tr2tog) made.

Double decrease: Work as for single decrease from *, but rep from * to ** once more into 4th st (4 loops on hook) before ending. Double decrease (tr3tog) made.

A single decrease in double crochet

A single decrease in half treble crochet

A single decrease in treble crochet

FOLLOWING PATTERNS

Crochet pattern instructions indicate, in abbreviated form, how many and what kind of stitches to work and where to insert the hook. They assume you are familiar with the basic stitches and other procedures and that you understand these abbreviations.

UNLESS OTHERWISE SPECIFIED:

- *Do not turn the work at the end of a row/round.*
- *Always count the turning chain as a stitch (see page 17).*
- *Work into the next available stitch in the previous row.*
- *Always insert the hook under both top loops of a stitch, unless it is a chain space or loop.*
- *The instruction, 1 dc, means work one double crochet into next sitch, and 5 tr means work 1 tr into each of next 5 sts.*
- *For a cluster, the instruction tr3tog or dtr5tog, means that each stitch is worked into a separate stitch, before joining.*
- *If all parts of the cluster are to be worked into the next stitch, the instruction would say tr5tog in next.*
- *The instruction to work "even" in a pattern means to work without any increasing or decreasing.*

MULTIPLES

In the stitch glossaries the pattern gives the number of stitches required in the row and the number of chains to work for the foundation chain in this way: Multiple of 5 sts plus 2, plus 2 for foundation ch. This means make 9, 14, 19, etc, chains in order to work with 7, 12, 17, etc. stitches.

BRACKETS [ ] OR PARENTHESES ( )

These are used in three distinct ways:
- *To simplify repetition – see Repeats (below).*
- *To indicate at the end of a row/round the total number of stitches that have been worked in that row/round. For example, (24 dc) means that the row/round counts as 24 double crochet stitches.*
- *To give information about different sizes.*

RIGHT SIDE/WRONG SIDE (rs/ws)

Even if a crochet pattern is reversible it is usual to define a right side. When working in the round, the right side is normally facing you. Where the work is turned between rows, instructions specify the first right side row. If you are directed to keep the right side facing you when working rows, fasten off at the end of each row and rejoin the yarn.

REPEATS

*Instructions in brackets are worked the number of times stated, ie: [ch 1, skip 1 ch, 1 tr] 5 times. A single asterisk marks the beginning of a pattern repeat sequence. For example *ch 1, skip 1 ch, 1 dc; rep from * across. A double asterisk indicates a smaller repeat in the main repeat sequence. The instruction: rep from * to last st means work complete repeats until one stitch remains.*

across	to the end of the row
alt	alternate
approx	approximate(ly)
beg	beginning
bet	between
bl	insert hook under back loop only. Example: bldc – back loop double crochet
ch(s)	chain or chain stitch(es)
ch sp(s)	chain space(s)
cl(s)	cluster(s)
cont	continue
dc	double crochet
dc2tog	work 2 dc together
dec	decrease
dtr	double treble crochet
dtr2tog	work 2 dtr together
fl	insert hook under front loop only. Example: fldc – front loop double crochet
foll	following
gr	group
htr	half treble crochet
htr2tog	work 2 htr together
in next	sts to be worked into same stitch
inc	increase
lp(s)	loop(s)
nc	not closed (see Clusters, page 73)

patt	pattern
p or pc	picot
rf	raised front. Example: rfdc – raised front double crochet
rb	raised back. Example: rbdc – raised back double crochet
rem	remaining
rep	repeat
rnd	round
sk	skip
sl st	slip stitch
sp(s)	space(s)
st(s)	stitch(es)
t-ch(s)	turning chain(s)
tog	together
tr	treble crochet
tr2tog	work 2 tr together
ttr	triple treble crochet
ttr2tog	work 2 ttr together
yrh	yarn round hook
*	Work instructions immediately following *, then repeat as directed, (see Repeats, page 24)
[ ]	Work or repeat all instructions enclosed in brackets as directed immediately after, (see Repeats, page 24)

FINISHING AND JOINING

For a polished, professional look, take special care when finishing and joining your work – its whole appearance and durability depend on it. Make sure all stray ends of yarn are woven neatly and securely into the wrong side. Seams can be sewn or joined with a crochet hook.

BLOCKING AND PRESSING

Cotton lace work usually needs careful pinning and pressing. Other crochet, particularly a textured piece, hardly ever requires this treatment. Pinning the article, misting with a fine spray, and leaving it to dry naturally may be just as effective. Tunisian crochet pieces may need more blocking (see page 82). Be sure to use rust-proof pins.

To join pieces of crochet work, it is often simplest to stitch them together, using matching yarn and a tapestry needle. But you can also use crochet stitches to join seams. These seams are strong and quick to work. Using slip stitch to join two pieces together gives the most invisible seam. Double crochet will form a ridge at the seam that can be a feature on the right side. The number of stitches to work per row end is the same as for edgings (see page 86).

When you are joining motifs, those with straight edges can be joined in the normal way. However, when there are many pieces, particularly squares and triangles, it is worthwhile connecting pairs of motifs in a continuous seam to avoid repeated fastening off (see page 27).

Piecing together different patches of crocheted motifs is a classic way to assemble a garment – as in this granny square top (see page 64–65).

SLIP-STITCH SEAM

Place the pieces right sides together. *Insert hook through both edge stitches, yrh and draw through to complete 1 sl st; rep from *, working loosely.

DOUBLE-CROCHET SEAM

Place the pieces right sides together (or wrong sides together for a visible seam) and work as for slip-stitch seam, using dc instead of sl st.

DOUBLE-CROCHET AND CHAIN SEAM

A useful variation on double-crochet seam, this is used when less bulk and/or greater flexibility is needed. Work 1 dc and 1 ch alternately.

FLAT SLIP-STITCH SEAM

Place the pieces edge to edge and wrong sides up. Work 1 sl st into each edge alternately. (See also alternative, below.)

ALTERNATIVE FLAT SLIP STITCH

A neat, flat seam may be made using the tops of stitches, as for example, with motifs made in the round. Lay the pieces edge to edge and right sides up. Insert the hook down through the top loop only of each corresponding pair of stitches and join with slip stitch.

Many motifs have a final round of picots or loops, and these may be used to join motifs to each other as that round is being worked. Typically the centre chain of a loop is replaced by a sl st or dc worked into a loop of the adjacent motif.

After joining, small motifs, which add decoration and strength, can be worked in the spaces between. The main motifs shown here are Flower Wheel, (see page 54). For the filler motifs, work a foundation ring of 5 ch (see page 53), then in round 1 [1 dc in ring, ch 2, sl st in motif, ch 2, 1 dc in ring] 4 times.

SIMPLE SASH BELT

Practice your basic crochet skills by making this simple belt to wear with jeans, a dress — virtually anything. You can dress it up with a fantastic selection of beads and trimmings.

❖ SIZE
One size

❖ MATERIALS
Yarn *Tweed-effect double knitting,
1 x 50g ball*
Hooks *One 5mm crochet hook*
Notions *Needle and thread,
beads and other trimmings*

❖ TENSION
10 sts and 10 rows = 6cm (2½in)

❖ SKILLS USED
*Chain (ch), p11; treble crochet (tr),
p15*

*See page 24–25 for pattern
abbreviations.*

STRING BIKINI TOP

This bikini top uses only double crochet, chain stitch, and slip stitch. The straps are made with a long string of chain stitches with double crochet added to each one for more strength. Pair it with shorts, jeans, or a sarong.

❖ SIZE
*One size: To fit 86–91cm
(34–36in) bust*

❖ MATERIALS
Yarn *Cotton glacé 100% cotton,
2 x 50g balls*
Hooks *One 3mm crochet hook*

❖ TENSION
24 sts and 21 rows = 10cm (4in)

❖ SKILLS USED
*Chain (ch), p11; slip stitch (sl st),
p11; double crochet (dc), p13;
rejoining yarn, p39*

*See page 24–25 for pattern
abbreviations.*

SIMPLE SASH BELT

Using double knitting and 5mm hook, ch 10; turn. Work in rows of tr until you have used up the whole ball of yarn. Fasten off.

FINISHING

Using needle and thread, stitch beads and patch motifs to the ends of the belt.

BEADED DETAILS

Stitching beads to the ends of this belt gives it extra visual interest and detail as well as adding some useful weight that will make the ends hang nicely when the belt is tied.

This belt has been made in a tweed-effect yarn that is mainly turquoise in colour, with little flecks of other colours. These shades are picked up in the beads that have been used. Fabric flowers motifs in the same colourway have been stitched along the ends.

Match your beads to your chosen yarn: they come in all shades, shapes and sizes, so you're bound to find something to suit.

BIKINI TOP
LEFT CUP

Using cotton glacé and 3mm hook, ch 36; turn.

Row 1: Ch 2, 1 dc in each ch to end; turn. Repeat this row 14 more times.
Row 16: Ch 2, 17 dc; turn.
Repeat row 16, 14 more times.
You will now have an L-shaped piece, measuring 15cm (6in) on the longer edges and 7.5cm (3in) on the shorter edges. Stitch the two short edges of the 'L' together, starting at the point where they meet at a right angle.

RIGHT CUP

Make this in the same way. Opposite side will be the right side.

FINISHING

Take the left cup: Starting at beginning of original foundation ch (this is inner edge), join yarn: Ch 2, dc to end; work 90 ch, (this is the neck strap); turn. Ch 2, 89 dc back along the ch. Then work 36 dc, evenly spaced, along the outer edge, to the outer corner; work 90 ch (this is the back strap); turn. Ch 2, 89 dc back along the ch. Then work 36 dc, evenly spaced, along the lower edge, until you reach the inner corner. Work 4 ch (to make the strap that joins the two cups), then join with a sl st to inner corner of right cup. Then work along the inner edge; work 90 ch (neck strap); turn. Ch 2, 89 dc, back along the ch. Then

CHANGING THE SIZE

To make the bra top slightly larger, simply work an extra row of dc all round after making up. An extra row of dc will also make the straps slightly wider.

work 36 dc, evenly spaced, along the outer edge, to the outer corner; work 90 ch (back strap); turn. Ch 2, 89 dc back along the ch. Then work 36 dc, evenly spaced, along the lower edge, until you reach the inner corner. Work 4 dc along the joining strap. Break yarn and fasten off.

BASIC STITCH VARIATIONS

You can achieve interesting textural effects by adapting the basic stitches. Inserting the hook into a different part of the work instead of into the top two loops of each stitch will change the look of a basic crochet stitch.

You can insert your hook in a variety of different ways. For example, you can work under one top loop at a time, between the stitches, or around the stem of the stitch. All crochet stitches can be worked with these variations, but some produce more interesting effects than others. As well as adding surface texture, these stitches will make a garment thicker and warmer. To begin any of these stitch variations, first make a foundation chain and work one row in your chosen stitch.

Stitch worked into back loop

Stitch worked into front loop

Simply working between two stitches can make an interesting texture, as seen in this cushion cover (see page 36).

WORKING UNDER ONE LOOP

By continually working into only the back loop (abbreviated as *bl*, as in *bldc*), you can create a pattern with a ridged effect. Working into only the front loop (*fl*) makes a less pronounced ridge with a horizontal line. This technique works well with the shorter stitches, for example double and treble crochet.

TO WORK INTO THE BACK LOOP

From the 2nd row onward work your chosen crochet stitch normally (for example, half treble crochet as shown here), but insert the hook into the back loop of each stitch.

TO WORK INTO THE FRONT LOOP

From the 2nd row onward work your chosen crochet stitch normally (for example, double crochet as shown here), but insert the hook into the front loop only of each stitch.

WORKING BETWEEN TWO STITCHES

This technique of working between the stitches of the previous row is quick and easy, and produces a slightly thicker fabric with a more open look.

TO WORK BETWEEN TWO STITCHES

From the 2nd row onward work your chosen crochet stitch normally (for example, treble crochet as shown here), but insert the hook between stems and below all horizontal yarns connecting stitches.

WORKING SPIKES

Spikes are arrow-shaped loops of yarn on the surface of the work. They are made by inserting the hook lower down than usual, for example, into one or more rows below the previous one (pattern instructions will always specify where).

TO MAKE A SIMPLE DOUBLE CROCHET SPIKE

Insert the hook into the base of the next stitch, yrh and draw it through up to the height of a double crochet (dc) in this row, (2 loops on hook) (right). Yrh and draw it through both loops. Double crochet (dc) spike made.

MORE BASIC VARIATIONS

MORE BASIC VARIATIONS

RAISED STITCHES

A raised effect can be achieved by working around the stems of the stitches in the previous row, either in the front (raised front, abbreviated *rf*), or in the back (raised back, abbreviated *rb*). Rows can be worked all in front or all in back, or alternatively one or more stitches around the back then one or more stitches around the front, to produce a large variety of different stitch patterns.

LINKED STITCHES

Longer stitches can be linked to each other down their sides to eliminate the space between the stems of the stitches. This creates an effect as if several rows of shorter stitches had been worked in the same direction at the same time.

Surprisingly easy variations on the basic stitches can create some very different looks in crochet (see page 50).

WORKING RAISED STITCHES

To make raised stitches you don't work into the top loops of the previous row, instead, you work into the stems of the stitches in the previous row. The stems are the vertical chains formed by the crochet, more obvious in the longer stitches.

TO WORK RAISED STITCHES AROUND THE FRONT

First work a row of your basic stitch, such as the treble crochet (tr) shown here. From the 2nd row onward, make each stitch normally, but insert the hook from right to left under the stem of the stitch below (left), on the front of the work. Wrap the yarn round the hook and pull through the stem, then continue as you would for the chosen stitch (right).

TO WORK RAISED STITCHES AROUND THE BACK

Work exactly the same as for raised stitches to the front, but insert the hook on the back of the work, from right to left around the stem of the stitch below (left). Yrh and pull through the stem, then continue as you would for the chosen stitch (right).

WORKING LINKED STITCHES

1 *Insert the hook down through the upper of the 2 horizontal loops around the stem of the last stitch made (shown here in double treble (dtr)), yrh.*

2 *Draw a loop through, insert the hook down through the lower horizontal loop of the same stitch, yrh and draw a loop through. (There are now 3 loops on hook.)*

3 *Insert the hook for the next stitch, yrh, draw it through the stitch only, [yrh and draw it through 2 loops only] 3 times. Linked dtr is made. Continue to the end of the row; turn.*

4 *To start a row with a linked dtr, treat the 2nd and 4th chains from the hook as the upper and lower horizontal loops of the last stitch made.*

BACK AND FRONT LOOP HALF TREBLE CROCHET

Multiple of 2 sts, plus 1 for foundation ch.

Row 1: Skip 2 ch, htr across, turn.

Row 2: Ch 2, *1 blhtr 1 flhtr; rep from * to last st, 1 htr, turn.

Row 2 forms the pattern.

BACK LOOP HALF TREBLE CROCHET

Any number of sts, plus 1 for foundation ch.

Row 1: Skip 2 ch, htr across, turn.

Row 2: Ch 2, blhtr across, turn.

Row 2 forms the pattern.

BACK AND FRONT LOOP DOUBLE CROCHET

Multiple of 2 sts, plus 1 for foundation ch.

Row 1: Skip 2 ch, dc across, turn.

Row 2: Ch 1, *1 bldc, 1 fldc; rep from * to last st, 1 dc, turn.

Row 2 forms the pattern.

ALTERNATE ROWS BACK AND FRONT LOOP TREBLE CROCHET

Any number of sts, plus 2 for foundation ch.

Row 1: Skip 3 ch, tr across, turn.

Row 2: Ch 3, bltr across, turn.

Row 3: Ch 3, fltr across, turn.

Rows 2 and 3 form the pattern.

HALF TREBLE CROCHET BETWEEN STITCHES

Any number of sts, plus 1 for foundation ch.

Row 1: Skip 2 ch, htr across, turn.

Row 2: Ch 2, *1 htr inserting hook between stems of next 2 sts and below all horizontal connecting threads; rep from * across, turn.

Row 2 forms the pattern.

1 x 1 RAISED TREBLE CROCHET RIB

Multiple of 2 sts, plus 2 for foundation ch.

Row 1 (wrong side): Skip 3 ch, tr across, turn.

Row 2: Ch 2, *1 rftr, 1 rbtr; rep from * to last st, 1 rftr, turn.

Row 2 forms the pattern.

TREBLE CROCHET BETWEEN STITCHES

Any number of sts, add ch 2 for foundation ch.

Row 1: Skip 3 ch, tr across, turn.

Row 2: Ch 3, *1 tr inserting hook between stems of next 2 sts and below all horizontal connecting threads; rep from * across, turn.

Row 2 forms the pattern.

DEEP RIDGED RAISED TREBLE CROCHET

Any number of sts, plus 2 for foundation ch.

Row 1 (right side): Skip 3 ch, tr across, turn.

Row 2: Ch 2, rftr across, turn.

Row 2 forms the pattern.

BACK LOOP SPIKED DOUBLE CROCHET

Multiple of 4 sts plus 1, plus 1 for foundation ch.

Special abbreviation

dc spike (double crochet spike): Insert hook into base of st, ie. 1 more row down, then complete dc normally.

Row 1 (right side): Skip 2 ch, dc across, turn.

Row 2: Ch 1, bldc across, turn.

Row 3: Ch 1, *1 dc spike, 3 bldc; rep from * across, turn.

Row 4: As row 2.

Row 5: Ch 1, *2 bldc, 1 dc spike, 1 bldc ; rep from * across, turn.

Rows 2 to 5 form the pattern.

ALTERNATING SPIKED DOUBLE CROCHET

Multiple of 2 sts plus 1, plus 1 for foundation ch.

Special abbreviation

dc spike (double crochet spike): Insert hook into base of st, ie. 1 more row down, then complete dc normally.

Row 1 (right side): Skip 2 ch, dc across, turn.

Row 2: Ch 1, 1 dc spike, *1 dc, 1 dc spike; rep from * to last st, 1 dc, turn.

Row 3: Ch 1, 1 dc, *1 dc spike, 1 dc; rep from * to last st 1 dc, turn.

Rows 2 and 3 form the pattern.

PEEK-A-BOO CUSHION COVER

This is an easy project for learning to crochet between the stitches. The stitch creates holes through which you can see the cushion. Start with a purchased cushion pad in a solid, bright colour. Trim the corners of the cover with pompoms if you like.

❖ SIZE
One size: 30cm wide and 41cm long (12x16in)

❖ MATERIALS
Yarn Double knitting 100% cotton,
4 x 50g balls colour A, 1 x 50g ball colour B
Hooks One 5mm crochet hook
Notions 30x41cm (12x16in) solid-colour cushion pad,
cardboard (to make pompoms)

❖ TENSION
21 sts and 9 rows = 10cm (4in) over pattern

❖ SKILLS USED
Chain (ch), p11; treble crochet (tr), p15; finishing and
joining, p26–27; raised stitches, p32–35

See page 24–25 for pattern abbreviations.

PEEK-A-BOO CUSHION COVER

Using colour A and 5mm hook, ch 39; turn.

Row 1: Skip 3 ch, 1 tr in each ch to end; turn.

Row 2: Ch 3, *1 tr, inserting hook between stems of next 2 sts of previous row and below all horizontal connecting threads; repeat from * to end; turn.

Next and all subsequent rows: Repeat row 2 until work measures 97cm (38¼in).

HOW TO MAKE A POMPOM

Cut two circles of card 10cm (4in) in diameter and cut out a hole 4cm (1½in) in diameter from the centre of each. Place the two rings of card together and wind the yarn around and around the rings until the centre holes are completely filled. Snip through the layers of yarn at the outer edge, slipping the scissor blades between the two pieces of card. Slip a 25cm (10in) length of yarn between the two card rings and tie firmly around the centre of the bunch of yarn. Slip off the card and you will have a pompom. Trim with scissors to neaten but leave the length of yarn long.

FINISHING

Lay the work flat and press lightly. Fold over 20cm (8in) at one end and 36cm (14½in) at the other end. The two short edges should overlap. Stitch the two long edges of the cushion cover together. Alternatively, work a row of dc along the long edges, through both layers, to make a decorative crocheted edge.

Divide the colour B yarn into four equal lengths and use to make four pompoms (see box below). When finishing the pompoms, leave long ends of yarn and use these to thread through the holes in the stitches at each corner of the cushion and knot the pompoms firmly in place. Insert the pillow into the lapped opening.

CHANGING COLOURS

Different coloured yarns are used to create stripes, geometric patterns and simple pictures in sharp contrasts or subtle gradations. Crochet stitches are generally larger and more varied than knitted ones and are perfect for overlapped and relief effects as well as multicoloured rows.

TEXTURED EFFECTS

Richly textured effects can be achieved using different types of yarn along with changes of colour. Multicoloured yarns create a new effect when combined with plain colours or textured yarns. Bouclé and mohair multicoloured yarns are shown worked together in this basketweave pattern sample.

When working with colour, you can use a single yarn, or strands of more than one to give both variegated colour and additional warmth. Yarns may be plain colour, two-tone, or patterned in different ways – heather mixtures, mottled, or multicoloured yarns.

Use single colours for one or more whole rows to create horizontal stripes. Carry the yarns not in use up the side of the work or cut them off and rejoin as required.

For blocks of colour, such as vertical stripes or intarsia, join a separate ball for each area or stripe, to avoid floats entirely. There is no need (as there is in knitting) to twist the yarns around each other at the point where they change over to prevent holes appearing.

When yarn is joined at the middle of a row, the yarn not in use is carried along the back of the work. This will form loops, or floats, which may catch during wear; these must be worked over every few stitches, or encased during right side rows.

CHARTS

Most multicolour patterns are shown as graphs, in which each square corresponds to one stitch – normally double crochet, since it is the smallest, squarest stitch. There are two main rules for following colour chart grids: always change to the next colour required just before you complete the previous stitch, and follow odd-numbered rows from right to left and even-numbered from left to right (a chart always represents the right side of the work).

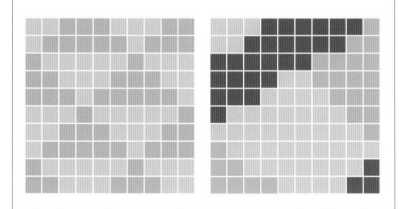

YARN ENDS

Provided you can do so without interfering with the visual effect, work over yarn ends whenever possible. Remember that all stray ends must finally be woven into the wrong side.

JOINING NEW YARN

When working horizontal stripes, change to the new yarn at the end of the row just before completing the last stitch so the new colour is ready to work the turning chain. If working in the round, work the last stitch with the old colour and use the new colour to make the joining slip stitch.

1 *Before you pick up for the last time to make the last stitch with the old colour, drop the old yarn and pick up the new.*

2 *Draw new yarn through to complete the old stitch – the working loop is now in the new colour. Before working the next stitch, make sure old yarn is kept to the wrong side of the work, or carried along the tops of the next few stitches so that it will become encased.*

CHANGING YARN

Change the yarns as for joining, just before you complete the last stitch with the old colour. Draw up the float in the new colour evenly, making sure the old yarn is appropriately positioned. Double crochet is illustrated here, but the same principle applies to all other basic stitches.

REJOINING YARN

Occasionally you will need to join yarn into a piece of crochet that has been fastened off, in order to make a fresh start.

1 *Insert the hook into the appropriate place. Start with a slip knot (or a simple loop, if you prefer) and draw this through.*

2 *Make the appropriate turning chain for the first new stitch (chain 3 for 1 treble crochet is shown here).*

FLOATS

To help the tension of floats be more even, catch them into the work every few stitches. When finished, cut in half any unacceptably long float yarns and weave them in.

STRIPED HALTER TOP

Great when you want to sparkle and shine at a party, this top is
dazzlingly different, easy to make, and takes only five balls of yarn.

❖ SIZE
One size: To fit 86–91cm (34–36in) bust

❖ MATERIALS
Yarn 4-ply lurex yarn, 3 x 50g balls colour A,
2 x 50g balls colour B
Hook One 3.25mm crochet hook

❖ TENSION
25 sts and 23 rows = 10cm (4in)

❖ SKILLS USED
Chain (ch), p11; double crochet (dc), p13; increasing,
p20–21; decreasing, p22–23; changing colour and
rejoining yarn, p39

See page 24–25 for pattern abbreviations.

STRIPED HALTER TOP

Using colour A and 3.25mm hook, ch 4;
2 dc in 3rd ch from hook; turn (3 sts).
Work in rows of dc, increasing 1 st at each
end of every row, until you have 9 sts.
Then join in colour B and work 2 rows,
increasing 1 st at either end of both rows.
Continue like this, working in stripes of 2
rows of alternate colours and increasing
1 st at the beginning and end of every
row, until you have 139 sts.

Work 14 rows without shaping.
To make the bra top, work 68 sts and turn.
Work in rows of dc, maintaining the
striped pattern, decreasing 1 st at each end
of every row, until you have 6 sts. Continue
on these stitches, in main colour and
without further shaping, for 96 rows, to
make halter strap. Break off yarn, rejoin and
work second side of bra top in the same
way; break off yarn.

BORDER AND STRAPS

Join yarn to point at base of garment.
Work 2 turning ch and 2 dc in same st,
then 69 dc, evenly spaced, up left-hand

YARN INFORMATION

This kind of yarn is quick to work
with but has a tendency to twist.
To prevent tangles, keep a rubber
band around the ball of yarn and let
out a little yarn at a time – about
30cm (12in).

side. Ch 84 (this is the back tie); turn. Ch 2
then work 83 dc back to start of ch. Work
19 dc up back edge. Then ch 84 (this is the
second back tie); turn. Ch 2 then work 83
dc back to start of ch. Work 31 dc up left
outer side of bra top. Work 95 dc along
edge of halter strap and 3 dc in corner st;
5 dc along end of strap; 3 dc in corner st;
95 dc down other edge of strap. Work 31
dc down inner side of bra top, 1 dc in
centre stitch, 31 dc up inner side of right
bra top; continue border around second
halter strap in exactly the same way as the
first, dc 31 down right outer side. Make a
third back tie in same way as first and
second; work 19 dc down right back edge.
Make a fourth tie, as before; work 70 dc
down right-hand side; join with a sl st at
2nd ch of t-ch. Fasten off yarn.

FANCY STITCHES

One of the great strengths of crochet is the versatility of the stitches.

Change the height of your stitches from row to row, and you

will see many different textures and stripe widths.

As you are working a row of crochet, making stitches of different heights will produce wave shapes and surface texture. Additional texture can be achieved by crossing stitches to produce a cable effect, or working them into different places. Making long stitches – reaching down below the level of the previous row and picking up around the post – will result in raised surface stitches, which look particularly striking when worked in contrasting colours.

RAISED SURFACE STITCHES

There are many variations of raised surface stitches, but they are all made in a similar way. The method shown below involves skipping stitches in the background fabric and working around the stem. The surface stitches must be longer than the background stitches. When skipping a stitch would result in a hole, work the raised surface stitch together with the background stitch, like a decrease cluster (see page 23). In this typical example the background is made with alternate rows of double crochet (dc) and treble crochet (tr).

Skip stitches (sts) in dc row and work raised surface sts in tr around the stem of the chosen stitch. Work at the front, alternately a few sts to left and then to right, inserting hook from right to left.

Leaving the last loop of each stitch (st) on the hook, work raised surface st, then background dc (there are now 3 loops on hook). Yrh and draw through all loops to complete the cluster.

SIMPLE CROSSED STITCH

1 *To make a pair of simple crossed stitches (treble crochet shown here), first skip 1 st and work 1 tr into next stitch. Yrh and insert hook into the previous skipped stitch.*

2 *Pick the yarn up and draw through, then yrh to work 1 tr.*

3 *The crossed tr wraps up and encases the previous tr.*

CABLE CROSSED STITCH (back)

1 *To begin cable crossed stitch, first skip 3 sts and then work 3 triple treble (ttr) normally (shown here worked on tr).*

2 *With hook behind sts, insert it from front. Work 1 ttr into each of 3 skipped sts.*

CABLE CROSSED STITCH (front)

Work entirely in the front of the previous stitches (holding them aside at the back if necessary) after inserting the hook, so as not to encase the stitches, as in Simple Crossed Stitch (left).

DOUBLE CROCHET AND SPIKE CLUSTERS

Multiple of 8 sts plus 5, plus 1 for foundation ch.

Special abbreviation spcl (spike cluster): Over next st pick up 5 spike loops by inserting hook as follows: 2 sts to right and 1 row down; 1 st to right and 2 rows down; directly over next st and 3 rows down; 1st to left and 2 rows down; 2 sts to left and 1 row down, (6 loops on hook); insert hook into top of next st in current row itself, yrh, draw loop through, yrh drawn through all 7 loops on hook.

Work 4 rows each in colours A, B, and C throughout.

Note: T-ch does not count as a stitch.

Row 1 (right side): Skip 1 ch, dc across, turn.

Row 2: Ch 1, dc across, turn.

Rows 3 and 4: As row 2.

Row 5: Ch 1, 4 dc, *1 spcl, 7 dc; rep from * to last st, 1 dc, turn.

Rows 6 to 8: As row 2.

Rows 5 to 8 form the pattern.

INTERLOCKING TREBLE CROCHET SHELLS

Multiple of 6 sts plus 1, plus 1 for foundation ch.

Work 1 row each in colours A, B, and C.

Row 1 (right side): Skip 1 ch, 1 dc, *skip 2 ch, 5 tr in next – called shell, skip 2 ch, 1 dc; rep from * across, turn.

Row 2: Ch 3, 2 tr in first st, *1 dc in 3rd tr of shell, 1 shell in dc; rep from * to last shell, 1 dc in 3rd tr of shell, 3 tr in dc, turn.

Row 3: Ch 1, *1 shell in dc, 1 dc in 3rd tr of shell; rep from * across with last dc in t-ch, turn.

Rows 2 and 3 form the pattern.

ALTERNATING RELIEF STITCH

Multiple of 2 sts plus 1, plus 2 for foundation ch.

Work 1 row each in colours A, B, and C.

Row 1 (right side): Skip 3 ch, tr across, turn.

Row 2: Ch 3, *1 rftr; 1 tr; rep from * across, turn.

Row 2 forms the pattern.

INSET FLOWER BUDS

Multiple of 10 sts plus 3, plus 2 for foundation ch.

Worked with colour A and with B and C for the flower buds.

Row 1 (right side): With A, skip 3 ch, 2 tr, *ch 3, skip 3 ch, 1 dc, ch 3, skip 3 ch, 3 tr; rep from * across, turn.

Row 2: Ch 2, 2rbtr, *ch 3, skip 3 ch, 1 dc in dc, ch 3, skip 3 ch, 3 rbtr; rep from * across, turn.

Row 3: Ch 2, 2 rftr, *ch 1, skip 3 ch, 5 tr in dc, ch 1, skip 3 ch, 3 rftr; rep from * across. Do not turn but work flower buds in B and C alternately over each group of 5 tr thus: Ch 3, tr4tog, ch 1. Bind off—flowerbud completed. Turn.

Row 4: With A, ch 3, 2 rbtr, *ch 3, 1 dc in ch at top of flowerbud, ch 3, skip 1 ch, 3 rbtr; rep from * across, turn.

Row 5: As row 2.

Rows 2 to 5 form the pattern.

CHEQUERED TREBLE CROCHET

Multiple of 4 sts plus 2, plus 2 for foundation ch.

Work 1 row each in colours A, B, and C.

Row 1 (right side): Skip 3 ch, 1 tr, *ch 2, skip 2 ch, 2 tr; rep from * across, turn.

Row 2: No t-ch, working into foundation ch over ch sps of row 1 *ch 2, skip 2 tr, 2 tr; rep from * to last 2 sts, ch 1, skip 1, 1 sl st, turn.

Row 3: Ch 3, working into last but-one row over ch sps of last row, 1 tr, *ch 2, skip 2 tr, 2 tr; rep from * across, turn.

Row 4: Working into last-but-one row over ch sps of last row *ch 2, skip 2 tr, 2 tr ; rep from * to last 2 sts, ch 1, skip 1, 1 sl st, turn.

Rows 3 and 4 form the pattern.

DOUBLE AND TREBLE CROCHET STRIPES

Any number of sts, plus 1 for foundation ch.

Work 2 rows each in colours A and B alternately, or 1 row each in A, B, and C.

Row 1 (right side): Skip 2 ch, dc across, turn.

Row 2: Ch 1, dc across, turn.

Row 3: Ch 3, tr across, turn.

Row 4: As row 3.

Row 5, 6, 7 and 8: As row 2.

Rows 3 to 8 form the pattern.

MULTISTITCH WAVE

Multiple of 14 sts plus 1, plus 1 for foundation ch.

Special abbreviations wave (worked over 14 sts): 1 dc, 2 htr; 2 tr, 3 dtr, 2 tr, 2 htr, 2 dc. reverse wave (worked over 14 sts): 1 dtr, 2 tr, 2 htr, 3 dc, 2 htr, 2 tr, 2 dtr.

Work 2 rows each in colours A and B alternately throughout.

Row 1 (right side): Skip 2 ch, *wave; rep from * across, turn.

Row 2: Ch 1, dc across, turn.

Row 3: Ch 4, *reverse wave; rep from * across, turn.

Row 4: As row 2.

Row 5: Ch 1, *wave; rep from * across, turn.

Row 6: As row 2.

Rows 3 to 6 form the pattern.

TREBLE CROCHET BLOCKS AND SHELLS

Multiple of 10 sts plus 7, plus 2 for foundation ch.

Worked in colours A, B, and C.

Row 1 (right side): With A, skip 3 ch, 5 tr, *with B, skip 2 ch, (2 tr, ch 2, 2 tr – called shell) in next, skip 2 ch, with A, 5 tr – called block; rep from * to last ch, 1 tr, cut B, turn.

Row 2: With A, ch 3, 5 tr over block, *with C, 1 shell over shell as follows: Skip 2 tr, 1 shell in 2 ch sp, skip 2 tr, with A, 5 tr over block; rep from * to last st, 1 tr, cut C, turn.

Row 3: With A, ch 3, with B, 1 shell in 3rd of 5 tr block, *with A, work 5 tr block over shell as follows: 2 tr, 1 tr in 2 ch sp, 2 tr, with B, 1 shell in 3rd of 5 tr block; rep from * to last st, with A, 1 tr, cut B, turn.

Row 4: With A, ch 3, with C, 1 shell over shell, *with A, 5 tr over block, with C, 1 shell over shell; rep from * to last st, with A, 1 tr, cut C, turn.

Row 5: With A, ch 3, 5 tr block over shell, *with B, 1 shell in 3rd of 5 tr block, with A, 5 tr block over shell; rep from * to last st, 1 tr, cut B, turn.

Rows 2 to 5 form the pattern.

CHEVRONS AND MOTIFS

The basic stitches can be combined with increasing and decreasing to create zigzags, chevrons, and curves. The same plain stitch, increased and decreased alternately at frequent intervals at the same place in each row, will create a zigzag shape.

Waves of chevrons are worked across a long foundation chain to make this unusual scarf (see page 48).

If you want to change the shapes of rows as you work, for instance so that zigzags alternate with straight rows or angles reverse, then you must use stitches of graduated heights at the same time as increasing and decreasing.

By simply using increasing and decreasing in several different ways, you can achieve a variety of different effects. You can create curves and zigzags within a piece of crochet and combine these with other stitches to get interesting shapes and textures. You can also use increasing and decreasing to shape motifs — making individual pieces that you can join together to create a rich patchwork.

Zigzags and straight rows are combined in the swatch above left. Make a diamond by crocheting an increase triangle followed by a decrease triangle (left).

SIMPLE CHEVRONS

In these patterns the same row shape is maintained and all rows are parallel throughout. If you are given the instruction to *work even* when working chevrons, you must continue increasing and decreasing as already established to create the chevrons, but keeping the same number of stitches in each row and the edges straight.

1 *Increase by working additional stitches into the same place.*

2 *Decrease by joining stitches together into clusters (see page 23).*

TRIANGLE MOTIFS

There are numerous ways of combining simple triangles (right) to make patchwork covers or bedspreads. These kind of bedcovers have long formed a large and popular part in traditional crochet.

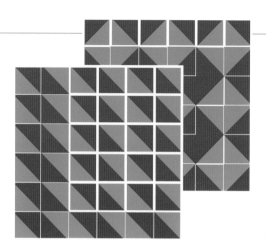

INCREASE TRIANGLE

Start with a foundation chain of 3 chains. Skip 2 ch, 2 double crochet (dc) in next, turn (3 sts – right side). Work 11 more rows in dc, making a single increase at end of every row and also at beginning of 4th, 7th and 10th rows (17 sts at end of Row 12).

DECREASE TRIANGLE

Start with a foundation chain the desired length of a triangle side – here 18 ch. Skip 2 ch, dc across to last 2 ch, dc 2 sts together (dc2tog), turn (16 sts – right side). Work 11 rows in dc, making single decrease at end of every row and at beginning of 3rd, 6th and 10th rows (1 st at end of row 12).

ZIGZAG SCARF

This woolly scarf has a zigzag pattern. Knit it in your own favourite colour combination to coordinate with a sweater or jacket.

❖ SIZE
One size: 25cm wide and 114cm long (10x45in)

❖ MATERIALS
Yarn Double knitting 100% wool, 2 x 50g balls colour A, 2 x 50g balls colour B
Hooks One 4mm crochet hook

❖ TENSION
8 rows = 10cm (4in)
1 pattern repeat = 6cm (2½in)

❖ SKILLS USED
Chain (ch), p11; double crochet (dc), p13; changing colours, p39; chevrons, p45

See page 24–25 for pattern abbreviations.

ZIGZAG SCARF

Using colour A and 4mm hook, ch 283; turn.

Row 1: 1 dc into 3rd ch from hook, *5 dc, skip 3 ch, 5 dc, 3 dc into next ch, repeat from * to end but finish with 2 dc (instead of 3 dc) in last; turn.

Row 2: Ch 1, 1 dc into same st, 5 dc, skip 2 dc, 5 dc, 3 dc into next dc, rep from * to end, but finish with 2 dc.

Row 2 forms the pattern.

Repeat this row throughout, working 2 rows in alternate colours (18 rows).

WORKING IN NEW COLOUR

In a piece of work like this scarf, where there are no seams, and no "right" or "wrong" side, it is important to hide yarn ends neatly or they will spoil the look of the finished piece. The colour not in use should be carried up the side of the work; to avoid a loop, twist the two coloured yarns together.

When you start a new ball of yarn, leave a 7.5cm (3in) tail of yarn, lay this across the top of the row to be worked, and work over and around it so it becomes trapped inside the new row of stitches. When the piece is finished, break off the yarn, leaving about 7.5cm (3in), and weave this neatly in and out of the stitches along the edge of the scarf. It is preferable to break the yarn, rather than cutting it, as cutting produces a blunt end which is more difficult to "hide".

CHANGING THE SIZE

To make a longer scarf, simply increase the length of the foundation chain. This chain can be any length, but should be a multiple of 14, plus 1, plus 2 for the turning chain.

To make a wider scarf, simply work more rows, until you have achieved the desired width.

If you are going to increase the size of the scarf, remember that you will need additional yarn.

TWENTY-SQUARES THROW

This cozy little blanket is made from twenty crocheted squares sewn together and given a contrasting border. The open look is achieved by working treble crochet stitches into the spaces rather than into the loops.

❖ SIZE
One size: 112cm wide and 135cm long (44x53in)

❖ MATERIALS
Yarn Aran weight 100% merino wool, 15 x 50g balls colour A, 6 x 50g balls colour B
Hooks One 6mm crochet hook
Notions Tapestry needle

❖ TENSION
Each square measures 23cm (9in)
11 sts and 7 rows = 10cm (4in) over the border

❖ SKILLS USED
Chain (ch), p11; treble crochet (tr), p15; joining seams, p27; changing colours and rejoining yarn, p39

See page 24–25 for pattern abbreviations.

TWENTY-SQUARES THROW

With colour A and 6mm hook, ch 28; turn.

Row 1: Ch 3, 1 tr in 4th ch from hook, (skip 1 ch, 2 tr in next ch) 13 times.

Row 2: Ch 3, (2 tr in space) 13 times, 1 tr in 3rd of ch-3 in previous row.

Row 3: Ch 3, 1 tr in space, (2 tr in next space) 12 times, 1 tr in next space, 1 tr in 3rd of ch-3 in previous row.

Rows 2 and 3 form pattern.

Repeat these two rows 7 times and then row 2 one more time. Break off yarn.

Make 19 more squares in the same way. Using a tapestry needle and length of yarn, stitch the squares together in 5 rows of 4 squares each.

FINISHING

Join in colour B at one end of a short edge. Work border: Ch 3, 111 tr along shorter edge of throw, 2 extra tr in last stitch, to turn corner; 140 tr along long edge of throw, 2 extra tr in last stitch, to turn corner; 112 tr along 2nd shorter edge, 2 extra tr in last stitch, to turn corner; 140 tr along long edge of throw, 2 extra tr in last stitch; join with sl st in 3rd of ch-3.

Work 6 more rows around border, working 3 tr into each corner st.

Note: When forming the border, you will sometimes be working along a horizontal row of the squares that make up the throw, and sometimes along an edge. When working along a horizontal row (in other words, a foundation chain edge or final row of a square), work 1 tr in each tr (28 sts along edge of square); when working along the side edge of a square, work 28 tr evenly spaced along the edge.

DIFFERENT SIZES

The throw pictured here is made up of 20 squares, each measuring 23cm (9in) and finished with a 10cm (4in) deep border. You could make your throw larger or smaller by making more or fewer squares and by making your border a different width.

PIECED WORK

Making a throw like this from separate squares joined together is a practical way to work. Individual squares are a manageable size and so can be worked on wherever you happen to be, so you don't have to carry a cumbersome piece of work around with you.

Though the throw pictured has been made in a single main colour, you could make squares from different shades and join them together for a multicoloured effect.

WORKING IN THE ROUND

Instead of being worked in rows, some patterns start with a centre ring and continue outward in rounds. When "working in the round," you stay on the right side at all times. This technique is used to make small, flat motifs and shaped items such as bags and hats.

MOTIFS

For the motif patterns on pages 54–55, unless otherwise specified:

- *Close the foundation chain ring by working a slip stitch into the first chain.*
- *At the beginning of each round work a turning chain to stand as the first stitch of the first pattern repeat (see the table on page 16 for the length of turning chains).*
- *At the end of each round close with a slip stitch into the top of this first stitch.*
- *Do not turn between rounds – right side is always facing.*

To create a flat item, increase regularly in each round. If you increase too much or too little, the fabric will curl or ripple. Shaped items like hats and bags are made with increases and decreases that force the item to cup or flare.

A flat piece made in the round may be any shape or pattern depending upon the position of the increases. Many different motifs are made using this technique (see pages 54–55). An enormous number of patchwork-style fabrics can be made by joining motifs together.

A tubular item like this tote bag (page 60) begins with a central foundation ring on the bottom. Increases give the bag its shape.

FOUNDATION RING

Working in the round starts with a foundation ring; the one most often used is closed by working a slip stitch into the first chain (chain foundation ring). When you want to be able to close any central hole in the fabric, use a yarn loop foundation ring.

CHAIN FOUNDATION RING

Make a short length of foundation chain as stated in the pattern instructions, for example, ch 5. Insert the hook into the first ch (left). Close the ring with a sl st (yrh and draw through – right).

YARN LOOP FOUNDATION RING

Make a loop in the yarn. Hold the bottom of the loop with the fingers which normally hold the work. Insert the hook through the loop, yrh (left) and draw through. Make the correct turning chain (chain 1 for double crochet) and work the first round into the loop ring, making sure you encase the short end of yarn (right). Close the round with a sl st. Close up the centre of the ring by drawing the short end of the yarn tight. Secure it by weaving it into the wrong side of the work.

WORKING IN JOINED ROUNDS

There are two ways to work in the round: making one continuous spiral or a series of joined rounds. In the latter case, each round is completed and joined with a slip stitch. Before starting the next round, a turning chain is made to match the height of the following stitches (even if the work is not turned between rounds). For the turning chain table see page 16.

1 *Make a foundation ring then work the correct number of chains for the t-ch, for example, ch 4 for dtr.*

2 *Insert the hook into the centre of the foundation ring; work stitches as required for first round.*

3 *To close the round, work a slip stitch into the top of the turning chain.*

4 *Before working another round, make the required turning chain.*

TREBLE CROCHET CLUSTER HEXAGON

Foundation ring: With A, ch 6. Work 1 round each in colours A, B, C, D, and E; join new yarn in ch sp.

Round 1: [Tr3tog in ring, ch 3] 6 times.

Round 2: [(Tr3tog, ch 3, tr3tog) in ch-3 sp, ch 3] 6 times.

Round 3: Join C in ch-3 sp, linking 2 pairs of cls, [(tr3tog, ch 3, tr3tog) in ch-3 sp, ch 3, tr3tog in next sp, ch 3] 6 times.

Round 4: Join D in ch-3 sp between 1st pair of cls, [(3 tr, ch 2, 3tr) in ch-3 sp, (3 tr in next ch-3 sp) twice] 6 times.

Round 5: Join E in ch-3 sp, [2 dc in ch-3 sp, 12 dc] 6 times.

POPCORN DIAMOND SQUARE

Foundation ring: Ch 8.

Special abbreviation pop (popcorn): 5 tr (see page 67).

Round 1: [1 pop, ch 5] 4 times.

Round 2: [1 tr, (2 tr, ch 2, 1 pop, ch 2, 2 tr) in ch-5 loop] 4 times.

Round 3: [3 tr, 2 tr in ch-2 sp, ch 2, 1 pop, ch 2, 2 tr in ch-2 sp, 2 tr] 4 times.

Round 4: [5 tr, 2 tr in ch-2 sp, ch 2, 1 pop, ch 2, 2 tr in ch-2 sp, 4 tr] 4 times.

SPIKE MEDALLION

Foundation ring: With A, ch 6. Worked in colours A and B.

Special abbreviations dcsp2 (spike double crochet 2 rounds below): Insert hook 2 rounds below st indicated, i.e. into top of round 1, yrh, draw loop through and up to height of current round, yrh, draw through both loops on hook (see Spikes, page 31).

pc (picot): Ch 3, sl st in dc first worked.

Round 1: With A, 16 dc in ring.

Round 2: With B, [2 dc, (1 dc, ch 9, 1 dc) in next, 1 dc] 4 times.

Round 3: [1 dc, skip 2 dc, (2 htr, 17 tr, 2 htr) in ch-9 arch, skip 2 dc] 4 times.

Round 4: Rejoin A in dc, [1 dcsp2, ch 5, skip 5, 1 dc, 1 pc, (ch 5, skip 4, 1 dc, 1 pc) twice, ch 5, skip 5] 4 times.

FLOWER WHEEL

Foundation ring: Ch 5.

Round 1: 12 dc in ring.

Round 2: [2 tr, ch 3] 6 times.

Round 3: Sl st in tr and in next ch, [(tr3tog, ch 4, tr3tog) in ch sp, ch 4] 6 times.

Round 4: [(2dc, ch 3, 2 dc) in ch sp] 12 times.

GRANNY SQUARE

Foundation ring: With A, ch 4. Work 1 round each in colours A, B, C, and D; join new yarn in ch-2 sp.

Round 1: [3 tr in ring, ch 2] 4 times.

Round 2: [(3 tr, ch 2, 3 tr) in ch-2 sp, ch 1] 4 times.

Round 3: [(3 tr, ch 2, 3 tr) in ch-2 sp, ch 1, 3 tr in next sp, ch 1] 4 times.

Round 4: [(3 tr, ch 2, 3 tr) in ch-2 sp, (ch 1, 3 tr in next sp) twice, ch 1] 4 times.

FLOWER POWER

Foundation ring: Ch 6.

Round 1: 12 dc in ring.

Round 2: [1 dc, ch 7, skip 1] 5 times, 1 dc, ch 3, skip 1, 1 dtr in top of first dc (counts as 6th ch-7 loop).

Round 3: [5 tr in ch loop, ch 3] 6 times.

Round 4: [5 tr, ch 3, 1 dc in ch loop, ch 3] 6 times.

Round 5: [tr5tog, (ch 5, 1 dc in next loop) twice, ch 5] 6 times.

Round 6: Sl st in each of next 3 ch, [1 dc in ch loop, ch 5] 18 times.

Round 7: Sl st in each of next 3 ch, [1 dc in ch loop, ch 5, 1 dc in ch loop, ch 3, (5 tr, ch 3, 5 tr) in ch loop, ch 3] 6 times.

RAISED TREBLE CROCHET SQUARE

Foundation ring: With A, ch 8. Work 1 round each in colours A, B, C, and D; join new yarn in ch-3 sp.

Round 1: [3 tr in ring, ch 3] 4 times.

Round 2: [3 tr in same sp, 3 rftr, 3 tr in next sp, ch 3] 4 times.

Round 3: [3 tr in same sp, 3 rbtr, 3 rftr, 3 rbtr, 3 tr in next sp, ch 3] 4 times.

Round 4: [3 tr in same sp, (3 rftr, 3 rbtr) twice, 3 rftr, 3 tr in next sp, ch 3] 4 times.

ROSE SQUARE

Foundation ring: With A, ch 6. Worked in colours A, B, and C.

Round 1: With A, 16 dc in ring.

Round 2: [1 tr, ch 3, skip 1 dc] 8 times.

Round 3: [Work a petal of (1 dc, 1 htr, 5 tr, 1 htr, 1 dc) in ch-3 sp] 8 times.

Round 4: With B, [1 dc between 2 dc, ch 6 behind petal of round 3] 8 times.

Round 5: [Work a petal of (1 dc, 1 htr, 6 tr, 1 htr, 1 dc) in ch-6 loop] 8 times.

Round 6: Join C in 2nd tr of petal of round 5, [1 dc in 2nd tr of petal, ch 6, skip 2, 1 dc, ch 6, skip 6] 8 times, omitting last 3 ch and working 1 tr in first dc of round instead to close round (counts as last ch-6 loop).

Round 7: [4 tr in same loop, ch 4, 1 dc in next loop, (ch 6, 1 dc in next loop) twice, ch 4, 4 tr in next loop, ch 4] 4 times.

PUFF STAR SQUARE

Foundation ring: Ch 4.

Special abbreviation puff: htr4tog in same place (see page 67).

Round 1: 12 tr in ring.

Round 2: [1 puff, (ch 1, 1 puff) twice, ch 5] 4 times, close round with sl st, sl st in next ch sp.

Round 3: [1 puff in ch sp, ch 1, 1 puff in next ch sp, ch 2, 5 tr in ch-5 loop, ch 2] 4 times, close round with sl st, sl st in next ch sp.

Round 4: [1 puff in ch sp, ch 3, skip (1 puff, 2 ch), (1 tr, ch 1) twice, 5 tr in next, (ch 1, 1 tr) twice, ch 3, skip (2 ch, 1 puff)] 4 times, close round with sl st.

Round 5: 1 dc in each ch sp and each st around, except 3 dc in 3rd of 5 tr at each corner.

SPIRAL HEXAGON

Foundation ring: Ch 5.

Note: This motif is worked as a continuous spiral without joining between rounds. Hint: mark the last dc of each round with contrasting thread.

Round 1: [Ch 6, 1 dc in ring] 6 times.

Round 2: [Ch 4, 1 dc in next sp] 6 times.

Round 3: [Ch 4, 1 dc in next sp, 1 dc in next dc] 6 times.

Round 4: [Ch 4, 1 dc in next sp, 2 dc] 6 times.

Round 5: [Ch 4, 1 dc in next sp, 3 dc] 6 times.

Rep for as many rounds as desired, increasing number of dc in each of 6 sections of each round as established. From round 10 work 5 instead of 4 ch in each sp. End with a ch sp then 1 sl st in next dc.

ADULT BUCKET HAT

These summer hats are colourful, fun, and comfortable – and very

quick and easy to crochet.

❖ SIZE
One size: 57cm (22½in)
circumference, to fit average head

❖ MATERIALS
Yarn *Cotton glacé 100% cotton,*
2 x 50g balls
Hooks *One 2.5mm crochet hook*

❖ TENSION
22 sts and 22 rows = 10cm (4in)

❖ SKILLS USED
Chain (ch), p11; slip stitch (sl st),
p11; double crochet (dc), p13;
increasing, p21; working in the
round, p53

See pages 24–25 for pattern
abbreviations.

BABY BUCKET HAT

Make a miniature version for a baby you love – perfect for keeping

the sun off delicate skin.

❖ SIZE
One size: 45cm (17¾in)
circumference, to fit average head

❖ MATERIALS
Yarn *4-ply cotton, 1 x 50g ball*
Hooks *One 2.5mm crochet hook*
Notions *30cm (12in) of narrow*
ribbon

❖ TENSION
24 sts and 21 rows = 10cm (4in)

❖ SKILLS USED
Chain (ch), p11; slip stitch (sl st),
p11; double crochet (dc), p13;
increasing, p21; working in the
round, p53; picots, p73

See pages 24–25 for pattern
abbreviations.

ADULT HAT

Using cotton glacé and 2.5mm hook, ch 6 and join with a sl st to form a foundation ring.

Round 1: Ch 2, 11 dc in ring, join with a sl st to 2nd ch of first ch (12 dc).

Round 2: Ch 2, 1 dc in 1st dc; *2 dc in each dc, rep from * to end; join with a sl st to 2nd ch of first ch (24 dc).

Round 3: Ch 2, 2 dc in next dc, *1 dc, 2 dc in next dc, rep from * to end; join with a sl st to 2nd ch of first ch (36 dc).

Round 4: Ch 2, 1 dc, 2 dc in next dc, *2 dc, 2 dc in next dc, rep from * to end join with a sl st to 2nd ch of first ch (48 dc).

Round 5: Ch 2, then continue in dc without shaping.

Round 6: Ch 2, 2 dc, 2 dc in next dc, *3 dc, 2 dc in next dc, rep from * to end join with a sl st to 2nd ch of first ch (60 dc).

Round 7: Ch 2, 3 dc, 2 dc in next dc, *4 dc, 2 dc in next dc, rep from * to end; join with a sl st to 2nd ch of first ch (72 dc).

Round 8: Ch 2, then continue in dc without shaping.

Round 9: Ch 2, 4 dc, 2 dc in next dc, *5 dc, 2 dc in next dc, rep from * to end join with a sl st to 2nd ch of first ch (84 dc).

Round 10: Ch 2, 5 dc, 2 dc in next dc, *6 dc, 2 dc in next dc, rep from * to end; join with a sl st to 2nd ch of first ch (96 dc).

Round 11: Ch 2, then continue in dc without shaping.

Round 12: Ch 2, 6 dc, 2 dc in next dc, *7 dc, 2 dc in next dc, rep from * to end; join with a sl st to 2nd ch of first ch (108 dc).

Round 13: Ch 2, 7 dc, 2 dc in next dc, *8 dc, 2 dc in next dc, rep from * to end; join with a sl st to 2nd ch of first ch (120 dc).

Round 14: Ch 2, then continue in dc without shaping.

Round 15: Ch 2, 8 dc, 2 dc in next dc, *9 dc, 2 dc in next dc, rep from * to end; join with a sl st to 2nd ch of first ch (132 dc).

Sides: Work 23 rounds in dc without shaping.

Shape brim: Ch 2, 9 dc, 2 dc in next dc, *10 dc, 2 dc in next dc, rep from * to end; join with a sl st to 2nd ch of first ch (144 dc).

Next round: Ch 2, 10 dc, 2 dc in next dc, *11 dc, 2 dc in next dc, rep from * to end; join with a sl st to 2nd ch of first ch (156 dc).

Next round: Ch 2, 11 dc, 2 dc in next dc, *12 dc, 2 dc in next dc, rep from * to end; join with a sl st to 2nd ch of first ch (168 dc).

Next round: Ch 2, 12 dc, 2 dc in next dc, *13 dc, 2 dc in next dc, rep from * to end; join with a sl st to 2nd ch of first ch (180 dc).

FINISHING

Pin or stitch crochet flowers to the hat for an extra flourish. See pages 92–93 for instructions on how to make flowers.

BABY HAT

Using 4-ply yarn and 2.5mm hook, proceed in exactly the same way as the adult hat, up to and including Round 12 (108 dc). Work 20 rounds in dc without shaping.

Next round: Ch 2, 7 dc, 2 dc in next dc, *8 dc, 2 dc in next dc, rep from * to end; join with a sl st to 2nd ch of first ch (120 dc).

Next round: Ch 2, 8 dc, 2 dc in next dc, *9 dc, 2 dc in next dc, rep from * to end; join with a sl st to 2nd ch of first ch (132 dc).

Next round: Ch 2, 9 dc, 2 dc in next dc, *10 dc, 2 dc in next dc), rep from * to end; join with a sl st to 2nd ch of first ch (144 dc).

Next round (picot edge): (Ch 4, sl st into same dc, sl st into next 2 dc) 48 times; fasten off.

FINISHING

Turn back brim, push ends of ribbon through from inside, between stitches, and tie in a bow.

MULTICOLOURED BAG

This everyday bag is made from hand-dyed cotton yarn that creates a striped look. Instructions on how to dye your own yarn can be found on page 94.

BEADED BAG

This evening bag is embellished with iridescent glass beads. The top has a fluted, picot edge worked in a double layer. Beads are threaded onto the yarn and worked into the stitches as they are formed.

❖ SIZES
  20cm (8in) long

❖ MATERIALS
  Yarn *Very fine (12-gauge) cotton,*
  1 x 50g ball
  Hooks *One 1.5mm steel crochet*
  hook

❖ TENSION
  33 sts and 30 rows = 10cm (4in)

❖ SKILLS USED
  Chain (ch), p11; slip stitch (sl st),
  p11; double crochet (dc), p13;
  treble crochet (tr), p15; increasing,
  p21; working in the round, p53;
  picots, p73

See page 24–25 for pattern
abbreviations.

❖ SIZES
  23cm (9in) long

❖ MATERIALS
  Yarn *4-ply cotton, 1 x 50g ball*
  Hooks *One 2.5mm crochet hook*
  Notions *90 beads, approximately*
  5mm diameter

❖ TENSION
  24 sts and 21 rows = 10cm (4in)

❖ SKILLS USED
  Chain (ch), p11; slip stitch (sl st),
  p11; double crochet (dc), p13;
  treble crochet (tr), p15; increasing,
  p21; working in the round, p53;
  picots, p73

See page 24–25 for pattern
abbreviations.

MULTICOLOURED BAG

Worked in the round, in one piece, starting from the base.

Using the fine yarn and 1.5mm steel hook, ch 6, join with sl st in first ch to form ring.

Round 1: Ch 2, 11 dc in ring, join with a sl st to 2nd ch of ch-2 (12 dc).

Round 2: Ch 2, 1 dc in next dc, *2 dc in next dc, rep from * to end; join with a sl st to 2nd ch of ch-2 (24 dc).

Round 3: Ch 2, 2 dc in next dc, *1 dc, 2 dc in next dc, rep from * to end; join with a sl st to 2nd ch of ch-2 (36 dc).

Round 4: Ch 2, 1 dc, 2 dc in next dc, *2 dc, 2 dc in next dc, rep from * to end; join with a sl st to 2nd ch of ch-2 (48 dc).

Round 5: Ch 2, 2 dc, 2 dc in next dc, *3 dc, 2 dc in next dc, rep from * to end; join with a sl st to 2nd ch of ch-2 (60 dc).

Round 6: Ch 2, 3 dc, 2 dc in next dc, *4 dc, 2 dc in next dc, rep from * to end; join with a sl st to 2nd ch of ch-2 (72 dc).

Round 7: Ch 2, 4 dc, 2 dc in next dc, *5 dc, 2 dc in next dc, rep from * to end; join with a sl st to 2nd ch of ch-2 (84 dc). Work 50 rounds in dc without shaping.

Next round (eyelets): Ch 3, 1 tr in next dc, *ch 1, skip 1 dc, 2 tr, repeat from * to end, ch 1, join with a sl st to 3rd ch of ch-3. Work 1 round of dc without shaping.

Next round (picot edge): (Ch 4, sl st into same dc, sl st into next 2 dc) 28 times; fasten off.

CORDS

Using the fine yarn and 1.5mm steel hook, ch 100, turn and work dc all along chain to end; fasten off. Repeat to make a second cord.

FINISHING

Thread one of the cords in and out of the eyelets and join the ends. Starting on the opposite side of the bag from where the first cords emerge, thread the remaining cord through the eyelets and join the ends.

BEADED BAG

Worked in the round, in one piece, starting from the base.

Using 4-ply cotton and 2.5mm hook, ch 20.

Round 1: Ch 2, 18 dc along foundation ch; 3 dc in last st, then work 19 dc back along opposite side of foundation ch, 3 dc in last st, join with a sl st to 2nd ch of ch-2 (44 dc).

Round 2: Ch 2, 19 dc, 3 dc in next dc, 21 dc, 3 dc in next dc, 1 dc; join with a sl st to 2nd ch of ch-2 (48 dc).

Round 3: Ch 2, 20 dc, 3 dc in next dc, 23 dc, 3 dc in next dc, 2 dc; join with a sl st to 2nd ch of ch-2 (52 dc).

Round 4: Ch 2, 21 dc, 3 dc in next dc, 25 dc, 3 dc in next dc, 3 dc; join with a sl st to 2nd ch of ch-2 (56 dc).

Round 5: Ch 2, 22 dc, 3 dc in next dc, 27 dc, 3 dc in next dc, 4 dc; join with a sl st to 2nd ch of ch-2 (60 dc). Work 30 rounds in dc without shaping.

Next round (increase): Ch 2, 2 dc in next dc, *1 dc, 2 dc in next dc, repeat from * to end; join with a sl st to 2nd ch of ch-2 (90 dc). Work 5 rounds in dc without shaping.

Next round (eyelets): **Ch 4, 1 tr in next dc, *ch 1, skip 1 dc, 1 tr in next dc, repeat from * to end, 1 ch, join with a sl st to 3nd ch of ch-4. Work 1 row of dc. Fasten off yarn. Thread beads onto ball of yarn and rejoin yarn to edge of work.

Next round (picot edge): *Ch 2, slip one bead along yarn, close to last stitch worked, ch 2, sl st into base of picot, sl st into next 2 dc, repeat from * to end (45 times in total – i.e. 45 picots, each with a single bead) and fasten off. Rejoin yarn to work 1 row below eyelet row, work 1 row of dc, then repeat from ** to make the second layer of the double-layered edging.

CORDS

Using 4-ply cotton and 2.5mm hook, ch 100, turn and work dc all along chain to end; fasten off. Repeat to make a second cord.

FINISHING

Thread the cords in and out through both layers of eyelets, as in the multicoloured bag, left.

TUBULAR TOTE

Here is a practical, go-anywhere, take-anything bag. It features bold stripes and is worked in the round.

❖ SIZE
One size: 30cm (12in) long and 66cm (26in) around

❖ MATERIALS
Yarn *Cotton glacé 100% cotton, 2 x 50g balls colour A,
1 x 50g ball colour B, 2 x 50g balls colour C*
Hook *One 3mm crochet hook*

❖ TENSION
22 sts and 22 rows = 10cm (4in)

❖ SKILLS USED
*Chain (ch), p11; slip stitch (sl st), p11; double crochet
(dc), p13; increasing, p21; changing colours and rejoining
yarn, p39; working in the round, p53*

See pages 24–25 for pattern abbreviations.

TUBULAR TOTE

Using colour A and 3 mm hook, ch 6, join with sl st in first ch to form ring.
Round 1: Ch 2, 11 dc in ring, join with a sl st to 2nd ch of ch-2 (12 dc).
Round 2: Ch 2, 1 dc in 1st dc; *2 dc in each dc, rep from * to end; join with a sl st to 2nd ch of ch-2 (24 dc).
Round 3: Ch 2, 2 dc in next dc, *1 dc, 2 dc in next dc, rep from * to end; join with a sl st to 2nd ch of ch-2 (36 dc).
Round 4: Ch 2, 1 dc, 2 dc in next dc, *2 dc, 2 dc in next dc, rep from * to end join with a sl st to 2nd ch of ch-2 (48 dc).
Round 5: Ch 2, then continue in dc without shaping.
Round 6: Ch 2, 2 dc, 2 dc in next dc, *3 dc, 2 dc in next dc, rep from * to end

COLOURWAYS

This tote bag has been made in light, clean colours – just right for summer days. For a change of mood, why not pick some hot bright reds and pinks – maybe teamed with a zingy yellow? Alternatively, go for more muted shades – earthy browns and leafy greens – and give your bag a more autumnal feel. And if you can't find the colour you want, try dyeing yarn to the shade of your choice (see page 94).

join with a sl st to 2nd ch of ch-2 (60 dc).
Round 7: Ch 2, 3 dc, 2 dc in next dc, *4 dc, 2 dc in next dc, rep from * to end; join with a sl st to 2nd ch of ch-2 (72 dc).
Round 8: Ch 2, then continue in dc without shaping.
Round 9: Ch 2, 4 dc, 2 dc in next dc, *5 dc, 2 dc in next dc, rep from * to end join with a sl st to 2nd ch of ch-2 (84 dc).
Round 10: Ch 2, 5 dc, 2 dc in next dc, *6 dc, 2 dc in next dc, rep from * to end; join with a sl st to 2nd ch of ch-2 (96 dc).
Round 11: Ch 2, then continue in dc without shaping.
Round 12: Ch 2, 6 dc, 2 dc in next dc, *7 dc, 2 dc in next dc, rep from * to end; join with a sl st to 2nd ch of ch-2 (108 dc).
Round 13: Ch 2, 7 dc, 2 dc in next dc, *8 dc, 2 dc in next dc, rep from * to end; join with a sl st to 2nd ch of ch-2 (120 dc).
Round 14: Ch 2, then continue in dc without shaping.
Round 15: Ch 2, 8 dc, 2 dc in next dc, *9 dc, 2 dc in next dc, rep from * to end; join with a sl st to 2nd ch of ch-2 (132 dc).
Round 16: Ch 2, 9 dc, 2 dc in next dc, *10 dc, 2 dc in next dc, rep from * to end; join with a sl st to 2nd ch of ch-2 (144 dc). Work 25 rounds without shaping; fasten off yarn.
Next round: Join in colour B and work 3 rounds without shaping; turn, and work 8 rounds; turn and work 10 rounds (this forms a textured stripe in the centre of the bag); fasten off yarn.

Next round: Join in colour C and work 30 rounds; do not fasten off yarn but start to make first handle: Ch 100, count 20 sts along top of bag and sl st to next st. Work back along ch, working 1 dc into each ch; sl st in dc next to 1st ch, then work back along handle again, working 1 dc in each dc of previous row; sl st to top of bag, then work 1 sl st in each of 26 sts along top edge of bag, to take you to the position where you begin the 2nd handle. Work the 2nd handle in the same way as the first; fasten off yarn.

HANDLES

Make handles shorter or longer, according to your needs, or simply work one wide shoulder strap from one side of the bag to the other, if you prefer.

PET BASKET WITH LINER

Sturdy but soft, this basket will become the favourite retreat of your

cat or small dog. The washable liner is crocheted with fabric strips

you cut from an old T-shirt.

❖ SIZE
One size: 34cm (13½in) diameter, 15cm (6in) high

❖ MATERIALS
***Yarn** Utility string, about 200m*
***Plus** One old T-shirt, cut into 12mm (½in) strips*
[see Making fabric strips, page 63]
***Hooks** One each 6mm and 7mm crochet hooks*

❖ TENSION
10 sts and 11 rows = 10cm (4in)

❖ SKILLS USED
*Chain (ch), p11; slip stitch (sl st), p11; double crochet
(dc), p13; increasing, p21; changing colours and rejoining
yarn, p39; working in the round, p53*

See pages 24–25 for pattern abbreviations.

PET BASKET WITH LINER

Note: the basket and the liner are each worked in one piece, in the round.

BASE

Using utility string and 6mm hook, ch 6, join with sl st in first ch to form ring.

Round 1: Ch 2, 11 dc in ring, join with a sl st to 2nd ch of ch-2 (12 dc).

Round 2: Ch 2, 1 dc in 1st dc; 2 dc in each dc; join with a sl st to 2nd ch of ch-2 (24 dc).

Round 3: Ch 2, 2 dc in next dc, [1 dc, 2 dc in next dc] 11 times; join with a sl st to 2nd ch of ch-2 (36 dc).

Round 4: Work 1 round in dc without shaping.

Round 5: Ch 2, 2 dc in next dc, [2 dc, 2 dc in next dc] 11 times, 1 dc; join with a sl st to 2nd ch of ch-2 (48 dc).

Round 6: Ch 2, 2 dc in next dc, [3 dc, 2 dc in next dc] 11 times, 2 dc; join with a sl st to 2nd ch of ch-2 (60 dc).

Round 7: Work 1 round in dc without shaping.

Round 8: Ch 2, 2 dc in next dc, [4 dc, 2 dc in next dc] 11 times, 3 dc; join with a sl st to 2nd ch of ch-2 (72 dc).

Round 9: Work 1 round in dc without shaping.

Round 10: Ch 2, 2 dc in next dc, [5 dc, 2 dc in next dc] 11 times, 4 dc; join with a sl st to 2nd ch of ch-2 (84 dc).

Round 11: Work 1 round in dc without shaping.

Round 12: Ch 2, 2 dc in next dc, [6 dc, 2 dc in next dc] 11 times, 5 dc; join with a sl st to 2nd ch of ch-2 (96 dc).

Round 13: Work 1 round in dc without shaping.

Round 14: Ch 2, 2 dc in next dc, [7 dc, 2 dc in next dc] 11 times, 6 dc; join with a sl st to 2nd ch of ch-2 (108 dc).

SIDES

Turn and work 14 rounds without shaping.

Next round: Ch 3, 1 dc in next dc, *ch 1 skip 1 dc, 1 dc in next dc, repeat from * to end; join with a sl st to 2nd ch of ch-3; fasten off yarn.

BORDER

Join in fabric strip; ch 2, 1 dc into 1st ch sp; *2 dc into next 1 ch sp, repeat from * to end; fasten off.

LINER

Note: As you come to the end of one fabric strip, join in another of the same or a different colour.

Using fabric strips and 7mm hook, ch 6, join with sl st in first ch to form ring.

Round 1: Ch 2, 11 dc in ring, join with a sl st to 2nd ch of ch-2 (12 dc).

Round 2: Ch 2, 1 dc in 1st dc; 2 dc in each dc; join with a sl st to 2nd ch of ch-2 (24 dc).

Round 3: Ch 2, 2 dc in next dc, [1 dc, 2 dc in next dc] 11 times; join with a sl st to 2nd ch of ch-2 (36 dc).

Round 4: Ch 2, 2 dc in next dc, [2 dc, 2 dc in next dc] 11 times, 1 dc; join with a sl st to 2nd ch of ch-2 (48 dc).

Round 5: Ch 2, 2 dc in next dc, [3 dc, 2 dc in next dc] 11 times, 2 dc; join with a sl st to 2nd ch of ch-2 (60 dc).

Round 6: Ch 2, 2 dc in next dc, [4 dc, 2 dc in next dc] 11 times, 3 dc; join with a sl st to 2nd ch of ch-2 (72 dc).

Round 7: Ch 2, 2 dc in next dc, [5 dc, 2 dc in next dc] 11 times, 4 dc; join with a sl st to 2nd ch of ch-2 (84 dc).

Round 8: Ch 2, 2 dc in next dc, [6 dc, 2 dc in next dc] 11 times, 5 dc; join with a sl st to 2nd ch of ch-2 (96 dc).

MAKING FABRIC STRIPS FROM OLD T-SHIRTS

This can be done so that you end up with one long, continuous strip. First cut off the T-shirt hem and discard, then, beginning at one of the side seams, start to cut around the body of the garment, 12mm (½in) from the raw edge. When you reach the starting point, do not cut off the strip you have made but continue cutting in a spiral around the garment until you reach the armholes, then snip off.

Round 9: Ch 2, 2 dc in next dc, [7 dc, 2 dc in next dc] 11 times, 6 dc; join with a sl st to 2nd ch of ch-2 (108 dc).

Round 10: Ch 2, 2 dc in next dc, [8 dc, 2 dc in next dc] 11 times, 7 dc; join with a sl st to 2nd ch of ch-2 (120 dc).

Round 11: Ch 2, 2 dc in next dc, [9 dc, 2 dc in next dc] 11 times, 8 dc; join with a sl st to 2nd ch of ch-2 (132 dc).

Round 12: Ch 2, 2 dc in next dc, [10 dc, 2 dc in next dc] 11 times, 9 dc; join with a sl st to 2nd ch of ch-2 (144 dc).

GRANNY SQUARE TOP

Granny squares are back! This patchwork top is pieced together from individual squares, opening up many possibilities for combining colours. You could try other square motifs; just adjust your hook size if necessary to get the correct measurements.

❖ **SIZE**
One size: To fit 86–91cm (34–36in) bust. Finished size 96cm (38in) around bust and 50cm (20in) from shoulder to hem

❖ **MATERIALS**
Yarn 4-ply 100% cotton, 1 x 50g ball colour A (yellow), 3 x 50g balls colour B (pink), 3 x 50g balls colour C (green). Cotton glacé 4 x 50g balls colour D (blue)
Hook One 2.5mm crochet hook
Notions Tapestry needle, buttons (pink, blue, and yellow)

❖ **TENSION**
1 square = 9cm (3½in) approx

❖ **SKILLS USED**
Chain (ch), p11; slip stitch (sl st), p11; treble crochet (tr), p15; joining seams, p27; changing colours and rejoining yarn, p39; working in the round, p52–5

See pages 24–25 for pattern abbreviations.

GRANNY SQUARE TOP

Note: At beginning of every round, work ch 3 in place of 1st tr.

MAKING A GRANNY SQUARE

Using colour A and 2.5mm hook, ch 5 and join with a sl st to form a foundation ring.
Round 1: (3 tr in ring, ch 2) 4 times; join with sl st to 3rd ch of ch-3). Break off yarn.
Round 2: Join in colour B in any ch-2 sp. [(3 tr, ch-2, 3 tr) in ch-2 sp, ch 1] 4 times. Break off yarn.
Round 3: Join in colour C in any ch-2 sp. [(3 tr, ch 2, 3 tr) in ch-2 sp, ch 1, 2 tr in ch-1 sp, ch 1] 4 times. Break off yarn.

Round 4: Join in colour D in any ch-2 sp. [(3 tr, ch 2, 3 tr) in ch-2 sp, (ch 1, 2 tr in ch-1 sp) twice, ch 1] 4 times. Break off yarn. Make 47 more squares in this way. Using a tapestry needle and length of colour D, stitch 10 squares together in a row. Repeat this three more times then stitch the four rows together to make the body. Add two rows of four to make the straps.

FINISHING

Join in colour B at front lower right corner in ch-2 sp. Work border: (3 tr, ch 2, 3 tr) in ch-2 sp, [(ch 1, 2 tr in next sp), ch 1] 18 times, (3 tr, ch 2, 3 tr) in ch-2 sp. This forms the border for the right front (buttonhole) edge. Continue in the same manner, around the neck edge, over the right strap, across the back, over the left strap, down the left front and around the lower hem, in exactly the same way, working (3 tr, ch 2, 3 tr) in ch-2 sp at outer corners. When you get to an inner corner, skip one of the ch-2 sp (at the corner of the square motif) and simply work 2 tr in the next ch-2 sp, on the adjacent square. Work a similar border around each armhole.

Sew buttons, evenly spaced down left front edge, and aligned with holes in border on opposite edge, which act as buttonholes.

DOG COAT

Make a matching coat for your dog – a kind of pooch poncho! Sizes will vary, according to the size of your dog, but use the one pictured as a guide. Join rows of squares to achieve the size and shape you desire, then add straps to fasten under the tummy and around the chest.

RELIEF EFFECT STITCHES

A relief stitch sticks out from the surface, creating texture. Popcorn stitch, puff stitch, bobbles and bullion stitch are examples of relief stitches. They are easy to crochet because they use the same skills as increasing and decreasing.

A relief effect is created whenever you work a stitch taller than the stitches on either side – for example, a double treble crochet in a row of double crochet. The taller stitch cannot lie flat, but sticks out from the surface.

Similarly, if you work more than one stitch into the same place and then join the group into a stitch at the top, the excess will stand out. The taller and greater the number of stitches in the cluster, the more pronounced the bobble will be. Variations can be made using different numbers of stitches and inserting the hook in different positions.

This hat uses raised bobbles to add texture and interest (see page 70).

POPCORN STITCH

1 Work 5 stitches into the same place. Remove the hook from the working loop.

2 Insert it from front to back under the top 2 loops of the first stitch in the group. Pick up the working loop again and draw it through. To make a popcorn stitch stand out toward the back of the work, insert hook from back through to front.

PUFF STITCH

1 Work a cluster of half treble crochet (htr). Yrh, insert hook into st, yrh, draw loop through loosely. Without tightening the other loops on the hook, repeat 4 times.

2 Yrh and draw through all loops on hook. To secure, leave last of 11 loops on hook, yrh and draw through the remaining 2 loops.

BOBBLE

1 Work a decrease cluster of 5 tr (or whatever amount you like) all into the same place, in a row made otherwise of dc. *Yrh, insert hook into st, yrh, draw a loop through, yrh, draw through 2 loops; repeat from * 4 more times always inserting hook into same st (6 loops on hook).

2 Yrh and draw yarn through all loops to complete. The bobble is more pronounced when worked during wrong side rows.

BULLION STITCH

1 Yrh, say 7 times, as if making a long stitch. Insert hook, yrh, and draw through st. Yrh, draw through all the loops.

2 Allow enough yarn to be drawn through the loops to give them enough room to stand up as far as you wish. Yrh once more and, taking care not to allow the stem of the bullion st to tighten, draw through to complete.

BOBBLE PANEL

Worked over 13 sts on a background of alt tr (right side) and dc rows.

Special abbreviation bob (bobble stitch): tr5tog in same place (see page 67).

Note: Work each rfdtr around tr st 2 rows below.

Row 1 (right side): 13 tr.

Row 2 (wrong side): 4 dc, 1 bob, 3 dc, 1 bob, 4 dc.

Row 3: 1 rfdtr, 1 tr, 1 rfdtr, 7 tr, 1 rfdtr, 1 tr, 1 rfdtr.

Row 4: 6 dc, 1 bob, 6 dc.

Row 5: As row 3.

Rows 2 to 5 form the pattern.

BULLION WAVES

Multiple of 10 sts plus 2, plus 1 for foundation ch.

Special abbreviation bst (bullion stitch): Made with (yrh) 10 times (see page 67).

Note: T-ch counts as stitch only on right side (bullion stitch) rows.

Row 1 (wrong side): Skip 1 ch, dc across, turn.

Row 2: Ch 3, *5 tr, 5 bsts; rep from * to last st, 1 tr, turn.

Row 3: Ch 1, dc across, turn.

Row 4: Ch 3, *5 bsts, 5 tr; rep from * to last st, 1 tr, turn.

Row 5: As row 3.

Rows 2 to 5 form the pattern.

CROSSED TRIPLE TREBLE CABLE PANEL

Worked over 19 sts on a background of tr.

Note: See page 43 for crossed stitches.

Row 1 (wrong side): 19 tr.

Row 2 (right side): 1 rfdtr, 1 tr, skip 3, 3 ttr, going in back of last 3 ttr work 3 ttr in 3 skipped sts, 1 tr, 1 rfdtr, 1 tr, skip 3, 3 ttr, going in front of last 3 ttr but not encasing them, work 3 ttr in 3 skipped sts, 1 tr, 1 rfdtr.

Row 3 (wrong side): As row 1, except work rbdtr instead of rfdtr over 1st, 10th and 19th sts to keep raised ridges on right side of fabric.

Rows 2 and 3 form the pattern.

TREBLE CROCHET BOBBLES

Multiple of 4 sts plus 1, plus 2 for foundation ch.

Row 1 (right side): Skip 3 ch, tr across, turn.

Row 2: Ch 1, 1 dc, *tr5tog in next, 3 dc; rep from * to last 3 sts, tr5tog in next, 2 dc, turn.

Row 3: Ch 3, tr across, turn.

Row 4: Ch 1, *3 dc, tr5tog in next; rep from * to last 4 sts, 4 dc, turn.

Row 5: As row 3.

Rows 2 to 5 form the pattern.

PUFFS AND RAISED CROSSES PANEL

Worked over 11 sts on a background of tr.

Special abbreviations puff (puff stitch): htr5tog in same place (see page 67).

nc (not closed): see Clusters page 73.

Row 1 (right side): 11 tr.

Row 2 (wrong side): *1 rbdtr, 1 puff, 1 rbdtr**, 1 tr; rep from * once more and from * to ** again.

Row 3: *1 trnc in first, skip puff, 1 rfdtrnc around next (3 loops on hook), yrh, draw through all loops, 1 tr in puff, 1 trnc in next, 1 rfdtrnc around st before previous puff crossing in front of previous rfdtr, yrh, and draw through 3 loops as before**, 1 tr; rep from * once more and from * to ** again.

Rows 2 and 3 form the pattern.

DOUBLE BULLIONS

Multiple of 6 sts plus 2, plus 1 for foundation ch.

Special abbreviation bst (bullion stitch): Made with (yrh) 7 times (see page 67).

Note: T-ch counts as stitch only on right side (bullion stitch) rows.

Row 1 (wrong side): Skip 1 ch, 1 dc, ch 1, skip 1 ch, 1 dc, * ch 2, skip 2 ch, 1 dc; rep from * to last ch-2 sp, ch 1, skip 1 ch, 1 dc, turn.

Row 2: Ch 3, 1 tr in ch sp, *1 tr, 2 bsts in ch-2 sp, 1 tr, 2 tr in ch-2 sp; rep from * across, working last tr in last dc, turn.

Row 3: Ch 1, 1 dc, ch 1, skip 1, 1 dc, *ch 2, skip 2, 1 dc; rep from * to last 2 sts, ch 1, skip 1, 1 dc, turn.

Row 4: Ch 3, 1 bst in next ch sp, *1 tr, 2 tr in next ch sp, 1 tr **, 2 bsts in ch-2 sp; rep from * to last 6 sts and from * to ** again, 1 bst in next ch sp, 1 tr, turn.

Row 5: As row 3.

Rows 2 to 5 form the pattern.

PUFFS AND DOUBLE CROCHET

Multiple of 4 sts plus 1, plus 1 for foundation ch.

Special abbreviation puff (puff stitch): htr4tog in same place (see page 67).

Row 1 (right side): Skip 2 ch, dc across, turn.

Row 2: Ch 1, 1 dc, *1 puff, 3 dc; rep from * across, omitting 1 dc at end of last rep, turn.

Row 3: Ch 1, dc across, turn.

Row 4: Ch 1, *3 dc, 1 puff; rep from *to last 4 sts, 4 dc, turn.

Row 5: As row 3.

Rows 2 to 5 form the pattern

POPCORNS AND TREBLE CROCHET

Multiple of 6 sts plus 1, plus 2 for foundation ch.

Special abbreviation pop (popcorn stitch): made with 5 tr (see page 67).

Work 1 row each in colours A, B and C throughout.

Row 1 (right side): Skip 3 ch, tr across, turn.

Row 2: Ch 1 (does not count as st), *1 dc, ch 1, skip 1; rep from * to last st, 1 dc, turn.

Row 3: Ch 3, *skip (1 ch, 1 dc), (1 pop, ch 1, 1 tr, ch 1, 1 pop) in next ch sp, skip (1 dc, 1 ch), 1 tr; rep from * across, turn.

Row 4: As row 2.

Row 5: Ch 3, tr across, turn.

Rows 2 to 5 form the pattern

DIAGONAL SPIKE PUFF

Multiple of 3 sts plus 2, plus 2 for foundation ch.

Special abbreviation spfcl (spike puff cluster): Yrh, insert hook in next st, yrh, draw through, yrh, draw through 2 loops, (yrh, insert hook from front in 3rd previous st, yrh, draw through loosely) twice (6 loops on hook), yrh, draw through all loops.

Row 1 (right side): Skip 3 ch, *2 tr, 1 spfcl; rep from * to last st, 1 tr, turn.

Row 2: Ch 3, *2 tr, 1 spfcl; rep from * to last st, 1 tr, turn.

Row 2 forms the pattern.

VERTICAL POPCORNS WITH RAISED DOUBLE TREBLES

Multiple of 11 sts plus 3, plus 2 for foundation ch.

Special abbreviation pop (popcorn stitch): made with 5 dtr (see page 67).

Row 1 (right side): Skip 3 ch, 2 tr, *ch 2, skip 3 ch, 1 pop, ch 1, 1 pop, ch 1, skip 3 ch, 3 tr; rep from * across, turn.

Row 2: Ch 3, 1 rbdtr, 1 tr, *ch 3, skip (1 ch, 1 pop), 2 dc in ch sp, ch 3, skip (1 pop, 2 ch), 1 tr, 1 rbdtr, 1 tr; rep from * across, turn.

Row 3: Ch 3, 1 rfdtr, 1 tr, *ch 2, skip 3 ch, 1 pop, ch 1, 1 pop, ch 1, skip 3 ch, 1 tr, 1 rfdtr, 1 tr; rep from * across, turn.

Rows 2 and 3 form the pattern.

BOBBLE HAT

This hat in a tweedy yarn features a decorative bobble pattern that
makes it look and feel chunky and warm.

❖ SIZE
One size: 58cm (23in) circumference, to fit average head

❖ MATERIALS
Yarn *Double knitting 100% pure new wool,*
2 x 50g balls
Hook *One 4mm crochet hook*
Notions *Tapestry needle*

❖ TENSION
16 sts and 9 rows = 10cm (4in)

❖ SKILLS USED
Chain (ch), p11; slip stitch (sl st), p11; treble crochet (tr),
p15; triple treble crochet (ttr), p15; increasing, p21;
working in the round, p53; bobble stitch (bob), p67

See pages 24–25 for pattern abbreviations.

BOBBLE HAT

SPECIAL ABBREVIATION

Bob (bobble): tr5tog in next st

BOBBLE PATTERN

Round 1: Ch 1, 1 tr, ch 1, skip 1 tr, 2 tr, 1 bob, * 2 tr, ch 1, skip 1 tr, 2 tr, 1 bob; rep from * to end

Round 2: Ch 3, then continue in tr. These two rounds form the bobble pattern.

Note: The hat is made in one piece, starting from the centre of the crown and working in the round.

COLOURWAYS

You could work the hexagonal crown in one colour, the bobble patterned sides in another and the rolled brim in another – a great way to use up leftover yarn from a larger project.

CROWN

Using double knitting and 4mm hook, ch 6 and join with sl st in first ch to form foundation ring.

Round 1: Ch 3, 2 tr into ring, *ch 3, 3 tr into ring, rep from * 4 times more, ch 3; join with a sl st to 3rd ch of first ch.

Round 2: Ch 5, (2 ttr, ch 2, 3 ttr) into first sp, *(3 ttr, ch 2, 3 ttr) into next sp, rep from * 4 times more, join with a sl st in 5th ch of first ch.

Round 3: Ch 3, 2 tr, *(2 tr, ch 2, 2 tr) into ch-2 sp, 6 tr, rep from * 4 times more, (2 tr, ch 2, 2 tr) into ch-2 sp, 3 tr; join with a sl st in 3rd ch of first ch.

Round 4: Ch 3, 4 tr, *(2 tr, ch 2, 2 tr) into ch-2 sp, 10 tr, rep from * 4 times more, (2 tr, ch 2, 2 tr) into ch-2 sp, 5 tr; join with a sl st in 3rd ch of first ch.

Round 5: Work 1 round of tr without any shaping (96 tr).

Now work 10 rounds following the bobble pattern, joining each round with a sl st in the 3rd ch of first ch.

BRIM

Work 9 further rounds of tr. Fasten off yarn.

FINISHING

Turn up the brim. Thread a tapestry needle with a length of the yarn and make a few small stitches around the brim, on the inside, to hold it in place.

SHELLS, CLUSTERS AND LACE

Crochet can create delicate work that is also strong and durable. Stitches and crochet techniques can be combined to make different shapes and openwork patterns. Colour changes can add to the finished effect.

You can make attractive patterns by grouping stitches together in shells or clusters. Shells are formed by working a group of stitches into the same place, whereas a cluster is made of several adjacent stitches joined together at the top. Work these closely together, or for a delicate look, increase the spacing. Combine shells and clusters with mesh techniques (see page 76–79) to create lacy work.

Use lacy effects in crochet to make garments with a light and delicate look (see page 74).

SHELLS

Shell shapes in crochet are made by working several stitches into one place. These stitches may be all the same, or of varying heights to create an asymmetric shape. Shells may also contain chains to create spaces. If no stitches are skipped, working more than one stitch into the same place will make an increase (see page 21). If groups of stitches are worked at intervals with other shells between them, no increase is created. See Interlocking Treble Crochet Shells, page 44.

CLUSTERS

A cluster is a group of stitches worked into one stitch or space then drawn together at the top with a loop. A shell and a cluster in combination can make a starburst.

1 *Work the required number of stitches, leaving the last loop of each one on the hook. These are sometimes called* not closed *(nc).*

2 *Yrh, draw the yarn through all the loops.*

LACE

Lacework consists of shells and clusters as well as meshes (see pages 76–79), single chains, and arches or loops, including picots. There are two ways of working over chains. In the first method, insert the hook in between the threads of a particular chain (see 1). In the second, insert the hook into the space underneath a chain or chain loop (see 2). The second method is quicker and easier, so use this unless otherwise instructed.

PICOTS

These single or multiple chain loops are anchored together for decoration. They are often featured in Irish crochet lace networks (see page 77), and are frequently used as edgings (see page 86). To make this simple picot (right) the instructions would be: *1 dc in ch space, (ch 3, sl st in 3rd ch from hook – called picot).*

LACY CAMISOLE

This camisole has a timeless quality, with its lacy stitch, tiny pearl buttons and slim straps. Pair it with jeans for a trendy, casual look or with dressy skirts or trousers for evening wear.

❖ **SIZE**
One size: To fit 86–91cm (34–36in) bust. Finished size 94cm (37in) around bust and 60cm (24in) from shoulder to hem

❖ **MATERIALS**
Yarn 4-ply 100% cotton, 3 x 50g balls
Hook One 3mm crochet hook
Notions 6mm (¼in) mother-of-pearl buttons

❖ **TENSION**
12 rows = 10cm (4in) over shell pattern
20 sts and 7 rows = 10cm (4in) over yoke

❖ **SKILLS USED**
Chain (ch), p11; double crochet (dc), p13; treble crochet (tr), p15; rejoining yarn, p39; shells and picots, p72–73

See pages 24–25 for pattern abbreviations.

LACY CAMISOLE

Note: The camisole is worked in one piece, with the edging and straps added. The cord is worked separately and is optional.

Using 4-ply cotton and 4mm crochet hook, make a foundation chain of 217 sts, plus 2 t-ch.

Row 1: Skip 2 ch, 2 tr in next, [skip 2 ch, 1 dc, ch 5, skip 5 ch, 1 dc, skip 2 ch, 5 tr in next] 17 times, skip 2 ch, 1 dc, ch 5, skip 5 ch, 1 dc, skip 2 ch, 3 tr in last ch; turn.

Row 2: Ch 1 (does not count as dc), 1 dc in first st, [ch 5, 1 dc in 3rd of ch-5 loop, ch 5, 1 dc in 3rd of 5 tr] 17 times, ch 5, 1 dc in 3rd of ch-5 loop, ch 5, 1 dc in 2nd of ch-2 in previous row; turn.

Row 3: [Ch 5, 1 dc in ch loop, 5 tr in dc, 1 dc in ch loop] 18 times, ch 2, 1 tr in dc; turn.

Row 4: Ch 1 (does not count as dc), 1 dc in first st, [ch 5, 1 dc in 3rd of 5 tr, ch 5, 1 dc in 3rd of ch-5 loop] 18 times; turn.

Row 5: Ch 3, 2 tr in 1st st, [1 dc in ch loop, ch 5, 1 dc in ch loop, 5 tr in dc] 17 times; 1 dc in ch loop, ch 5, 1 dc in ch loop, 3 tr in last st.

Rows 2 to 5 form the shell pattern. Repeat these rows until work measures 24cm (9½in).

Next row: Work 1 tr into each ch of previous row; skip each dc; 180 tr worked.

Next row: Work 1 tr into each tr of previous row.

Repeat last row 11 more times. Break off yarn.

BORDER AND STRAPS

Rejoin yarn to bottom corner of left front and work 81 dc, evenly spaced, up left front, then work 2 more dc in last st to turn corner. Work 26 dc, ch 80 (for left strap), skip 40 tr and rejoin with a sl st to next tr. Work 48 dc, ch 80 (for right strap), skip 40 tr and rejoin with a sl st to next tr. Work 26 dc. Work 2 more dc in last st to turn corner, then work 81 dc, evenly spaced, down right front; turn.

For the buttonholes; ch 2 (counts as 1st dc), [ch 2, skip 2 sts from previous row, 5 dc] 11 times, ch 2, skip 2 sts from previous row, 1 dc; work 2 more dc in last st to turn corner, then continue in dc around border to top of left edge and turn (do not work 2nd row of dc down left edge). Next row (picot border): [Ch 4, sl st into same st, 2 dc] repeat across top, over left strap, across back, over right strap, along right top edge and down right-hand edge. Fasten off.

FINISHING

Sew buttons on left front to correspond with buttonholes.

DRAWSTRING

Make flat cord, 76cm (30in) long (see pages 90–91). Weave it in and out of ch loops below bustline.

COLOURWAYS

The choice of dusky pink yarn is fresh and feminine. But you could make this pretty top in any colour – in primrose yellow for a sunny summer top, or in black yarn with contrasting red border for a really sophisticated effect.

FILET MESH

Fine yarns and narrow hooks can create delicate openwork fabric. Various techniques have evolved, which you can use to make a range of different patterns, all of which have a lacy look.

Filet crochet creates an open, lacy fabric. A series of squares forms a mesh. Patterns are made by leaving some squares of the mesh open (spaces) and filling others in (blocks). This technique can make geometric patterns and shapes like birds and flowers. Filet crochet is used for edgings as well as for tablecloths, curtains and clothes.

CHARTS

Pattern instructions for filet crochet usually come on graph paper. Unless otherwise stated, read odd rows of a chart from right to left, even rows from left to right. You can usually adapt and use any squared chart as a pattern for filet work.

On filet charts, the spaces are represented by blank squares and the blocks by filled-in squares. The filet ground's vertical stitches are usually treble crochet and the horizontal bars ch-2 spaces. Occasional special features called bars and lacets are drawn as they look.

If a filet chart has 1 ch for the spaces, the squares become narrow rectangles

A mesh with ch-1 spaces and vertical stitches (tr) worked into the ch sps of the previous row gives a different effect

FILET MESH

To make a simple filet mesh of alternating blocks and spaces, first make a foundation chain: Make a multiple of 3 ch for each square required (which in turn will be a multiple of the number of squares in the pattern repeat), plus 1. Add 4 if the first square is a space, but only 2 if it is a block.

1 *To begin the first row with a space: Skip 7 ch, then work 1 tr.*

2 *To begin the first row with a block: Skip 3 ch, then work 3 tr.*

3 *Thereafter, work each space as: Ch 2, skip 2, 1 tr. Work each block as: 3 tr.*

4 *From row 2, at the beginning of each row, ch 3 to count as the edge stitch (tr), skip the first tr, and then, for each space, ch 2, skip 2 ch (or next 2 tr of a block), 1 tr in next tr; and for each block, work 2 tr in ch-2 sp (or in next 2 tr of a block), 1 tr in next tr.*

BARS AND LACETS

A lacet is a variation of filet mesh. A bar is normally worked over the top of each lacet in the mesh. Each structure occupies 2 squares of the pattern and is usually worked alternately.

1 *To make a lacet: Ch 3, skip 2, 1 dc, ch 3, skip 2, 1 tr.*

2 *To make a bar: Ch 5, skip lacet (or 2 squares), 1 tr.*

CLONES KNOTS

These knots can be used to embellish filet mesh. They are named for an Irish town that was an early centre for lace making.

1 *To make the knot: Ch 3, *yrh, take hook under ch loop just made, yrh, bring hook back again over ch loop; repeat from * 4 more times (there are now 9 loops on the hook).*

2 *Yrh and draw through all loops, slip stitch (sl st) in 1st of ch-3.*

BLOCK, BAR AND LACET

Multiple of 6 sts plus 1, plus 2 for foundation ch.

Row 1 (right side): Skip 3 ch, tr across, turn.

Row 2: Ch 3, skip first tr, *ch 5, skip 5, 1 tr; rep from * across, turn.

Row 3: Ch 3, skip first tr, *ch 3, 1 dc in ch loop, ch 3, – called lacet, 1 tr in tr; rep from * across, turn.

Row 4: Ch 3, skip first tr, *ch 5, skip lacet, 1 tr; rep from * across, turn.

Row 5: Ch 3, *5 tr in ch loop, 1 tr in tr; rep from * across, turn.
Rows 2 to 5 form the pattern.

BASIC TRELIS

Multiple of 4 sts plus 2, plus 4 for foundation ch.

Row 1 (right side): Skip 5 ch, 1 dc, *ch 5, skip 3 ch, 1 dc; rep from * across, turn.

Row 2: *Ch 5, 1 dc in 5 ch loop; rep from * across, turn.
Row 2 forms the pattern.

PUFF TRELIS

Multiple of 3 sts plus 1, plus 1 for foundation ch.

Special abbreviation puff V st: [htr3tog, ch 3, htr3tog] in same place.

Row 1 (right side): Skip 1 ch, 1 dc, *ch 3, skip 2 ch, 1 dc; rep from * across, turn.

Row 2: Ch 4, 1 dc in ch loop, *ch 3, 1 dc in ch loop; rep from * across, ending ch 1, 1 tr in last st, turn.

Row 3: Ch 3,*1 puff V st in dc; rep from * across, ending 1 sc in t-ch loop, turn.
Rows 2 and 3 form the pattern.

DOUBLE CROCHET NETWORK

Multiple of 8 sts plus 1, plus 1 for foundation ch.

Note: t-ch does not count as st, except on row 4, 10, etc.

Row 1 (right side): Skip 1 ch, 3 dc, *ch 5, skip 3 ch, 5 dc; rep from * across, omitting 2 of 5 dc at end of last rep, turn.

Row 2: Ch 1, 1 dc, *1 dc, ch 3, 1 dc in ch-5 loop, ch 3, skip 1 dc, 2 dc; rep from * across, turn.

Row 3: Ch 1, 1 dc, *ch 3, 1 dc in ch-3 sp, 1 dc, 1 dc in ch-3 sp, ch 3, skip 1 dc, 1 dc; rep from * across, turn.

Row 4: Ch 5 (counts as 1 tr and 2 ch), * 1 dc in ch-3 sp, 3 dc, 1 dc in ch-3 sp **, ch 5; rep from * to 2nd last ch-3 sp and from * to ** again, ch 2, 1 tr in last dc, turn.

Row 5: Ch 1, 1 dc, *ch 3, skip 1 dc, 3 dc, ch 3, skip 1 dc, 1 dc in ch-5 loop; rep from * across, turn.

Row 6: Ch 1, 1 dc, *1 dc in ch-3 sp, ch 3, skip 1 dc, 1 dc, ch 3, skip 1 dc, 1 dc in ch-3 sp, 1 dc; rep from * across, turn.

Row 7: Ch 1, 1 dc, *1 dc, 1 dc in ch-3 sp, ch 5, 1 dc in ch-3 sp, 2 dc; rep from * across, turn.
Rows 2 to 7 form the pattern.

FOUNTAIN NETWORK

Multiple of 12 sts plus 5, plus 1 for foundation ch.

Row 1 (right side): Skip 1 ch, 1 dc, *ch 5, skip 3 ch, 1 dc, ch 2, skip 3 ch, 5 tr in next, ch 2, skip 3 ch, 1 dc; rep from * to last 4 ch, ch 5, skip 3 ch, 1 dc, turn.

Row 2: Ch 5 (counts as 1 tr and 2 ch), *1 dc in ch-5 loop, ch 2, skip 2 ch, 1 tr in tr, [ch 1, 1 tr] 4 times, ch 2, skip 2 ch; rep from * to last ch-5 loop, 1 dc in ch-5 loop, ch 2, 1 tr in dc, turn.

Row 3: Ch 4 (counts as 1 tr and 1 ch), 1 tr in first st, *skip [2 ch, 1 dc, 2 ch], 1 tr in tr, [ch 2, skip

1 ch, 1 tr] 4 times; rep from * ending skip [2 ch, 1 dc, 2 ch], [1 tr, ch 1, 1 tr] in t-ch loop, turn.

Row 4: Ch 1 (does not count as dc), 1 dc, skip [1 ch, 2 tr], *ch 5, 1 dc in ch-2 sp, ch 2, skip [1 tr, 2 ch], 5 tr in tr, ch 2, skip [2 ch, 1 tr], 1 dc in ch-2 sp; rep from * ending ch 5, 1 dc in t-ch loop, turn.

Rows 2, 3, and 4 form the pattern.

FILET ROSE INSERTION

Foundation: Ch 60.

Row 1 (right side): Skip 3 ch, 3 tr, [ch 2, skip 2, 1 tr] 17 times, 3 tr, turn (19 squares).

Follow chart from row 2 for pattern, repeating rows 3 to 16 as required.

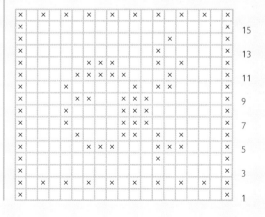

FILET DIAMOND BORDER

Foundation: Ch 36.

Note: For multiple increases and decreases see pages 20 to 23.

Row 1 (right side): Skip 3 ch, 3 tr; [ch 2, skip 2, 1 tr] twice, 3 tr [ch 2, skip 2, 1 tr] 5 times, [3 tr] twice, turn.

Follow chart from row 2 for pattern, repeating rows 2 to 12 as required.

MESH COVER-UP

Seamless and lightweight, this pullover can be slipped on over a bikini or strap top. It is shown in a yarn that looks like denim and goes great with jeans.

❖ SIZE
One size: To fit 86–91cm (34–36in) bust. Finished size 95cm (37½in) around bust and 51cm (20in) from shoulder to hem.

❖ MATERIALS
***Yarn** Denim-look double knitting 100% cotton, 8 x 50g balls*
***Hooks** One 4mm crochet hook*
***Notions** Tapestry needle*

❖ TENSION
9 loops and 18 rows = 20cm (8in) over trellis pattern 19 sts = 10cm (4in) over hem

❖ SKILLS USED
Chain (ch), p11; double crochet (dc), p13; joining seams, p27; rejoining yarn, p39; working in the round, p53; basic trellis pattern, p78

See pages 24–25 for pattern abbreviations.

MESH COVER-UP

Note: The sweater is worked in one piece, in the round, starting with the lower edge, so back and front are worked together.

Using cotton yarn and 4mm hook, ch 212, join with sl st in first ch to form ring.
Round 1: Ch 2, dc in each ch.
Repeat round 1 two more times.
Round 4: Ch 5, skip 3, *1 dc, ch 5, skip 3, rep from * to end; join with a dc in first ch loop.
Round 5: *Ch 5, 1 dc in ch loop, rep from * to last loop; ch 5 and join with a dc in first ch loop.
Round 5 forms the basic trellis pattern. Repeat this 28 more times.

ALTERNATIVE IDEAS

Instead of adding sleeves, you could make a vest. Simply complete the main part of garment and join at the shoulders. Leave it as it is or work a single row of dc around the armholes for a neat finish.

To make a longer or shorter sweater, simply work more or fewer rounds before shaping the back and front.

YARN AND COLOUR IDEAS

Make this pullover in a gold or silver glittery yarn for an evening cover-up to wear over a strappy dress or a skimpy top and trousers. Or make it in a bright cotton for beach wear over a swimming suit or bikini.

To shape the back, work 17 loops in basic trellis pattern and turn; **work 4 more rows of 17 loops.
Next row: Ch 5, dc in next ch loop; *ch 4, dc in next ch loop, rep from * until last loop; ch 5, dc in loop; turn; work 2 more rows like this.
Next row: Ch 5, dc in next ch loop; *ch 3, dc in next ch loop, rep from * until last loop; ch 5, dc in loop; turn; work 2 more rows like this.
Next row: Ch 5, dc in next ch loop; *ch 2, dc in next ch loop, rep from * until last loop; ch 5, dc in loop; turn; work 2 more rows like this. Fasten off yarn.
To shape the front, count 4 loops from beginning of back shaping and rejoin yarn; work 17 loops in basic trellis pattern and turn, then proceed from ** in exactly the same way as back.

SLEEVES

Using a tapestry needle and length of yarn, stitch the front and back together at shoulders. Rejoin yarn at one shoulder and work in basic trellis pattern around armhole (ch 5, 1 dc in each ch loop); 20 loops.
To shape sleeve, working from shoulder to wrist in rounds: Work 9 rounds of ch 5, 1 dc; 10 rounds of ch 4, 1 dc; 22 rounds of ch 3, 1 dc; 10 rounds of ch 2, 1 dc; 2 rounds of ch 1, 1 dc. Fasten off yarn.
Repeat for second sleeve.

Note: Some denim-look yarns can shrink after the first wash, making the garment shorter in length. The colour will also fade after washing.

TUNISIAN CROCHET

Tunisian crochet (sometimes called Afghan stitch) is worked with a special hook that is longer than usual, has a uniform diameter, and has a knob (or sometimes another hook) at the other end.

FINISHING TECHNIQUES

When you've finished a piece of Tunisian crichet, you may find that the edges curl. To combat this you need to block and press your work. Lay the piece out flat, wrong side up, on a padded surface. Smooth it out and pin around the edges, making sure you don't stretch the work out of shape. Cover the piece with a damp cloth and press lightly, with the iron on a warm setting. Alternatively, hold a steaming iron close to the surface, but not actually touching.

The Tunisian crochet technique is a cross between knitting and crochet. The finished work resembles knitting, but the stitches are thicker and firmer. Plain, textured, multicoloured and openwork patterns are possible.

For Tunisian crochet, you will use a hook at least two sizes larger than you would ordinarily use with the same yarn in regular crochet. Unless a double-ended hook is used, the work is never turned and so the right side is always facing.

The odd-numbered rows are worked from right to left, as loops are picked up and retained on the hook. In the even-numbered rows, the loops are worked off again from left to right.

Tunisian crochet is ideal when you want to create something that's sturdy and hardwearing, like this shoulder bag (see page 84).

| # FOUNDATION ROW

You should make a foundation chain with the same number of chains as the number of stitches required in the finished row, plus 1 chain for turning.

1 *To make row one (forward row): Make a foundation chain. Skip 1 ch, *insert the hook in the next ch, yrh, draw the loop through the ch only and keep the loop on the hook.*

2 *Repeat from * across. Do not turn the work at the end.*

3 *To make row two (return row): Yrh, draw through 1 loop only, *yrh, draw through 2 loops; rep from * across until 1 loop remains on the hook. Do not turn the work at the end.*

4 *These two rows make the finished foundation row – the basis of most Tunisian crochet patterns.*

TUNISIAN SIMPLE STITCH

Work the basic forward and return foundation row.

*Forward (row 3 and all odd rows): Count loop on hook as first st and start in 2nd st. *Insert hook at front and from right to left around single front vertical yarn, yrh, draw through and keep on hook; rep from * across. Do not turn.*

Return (even rows): Same as row two (return row).

TUNISIAN KNIT STITCH

Work the basic forward and return foundation row.

*Forward (row 3 and all odd rows): Count loop on hook as first st and start in 2nd st. *Insert hook from front through fabric and below chs formed by previous return row to right of front vertical yarn and left of back yarn of same loop, yrh, draw loop through and keep on hook; rep from * across. Do not turn.*

Return: (even rows): Same as row two (return row).

HARDWORKING SHOULDER BAG

If you put your bags to the test, try this sturdy pattern made
with Tunisian crochet. The bag is cleverly embellished with
rows of cross-stitches.

❖ SIZE
*One size: 17cm (6¾in) wide, 20cm (8in) long and 3.5cm
(1⅜in) deep*

❖ MATERIALS
Yarn *Cotton glacé 100% cotton, 2 x 50g balls in
colour A, 1 x 50g ball contrasting colour B (for border and
embroidery), small amounts of contrasting colour C
(for embroidery)*
Hook *One 3.5mm Tunisian crochet hook*
Notions *Tapestry needle*

❖ TENSION
24 sts and 24 rows = 10cm (4in)

❖ SKILLS USED
*Chain (ch), p11; slip stitch (sl st), p11; double crochet
(dc), p13; joining seams, p27; changing colours, p39;
Tunisian simple stitch, p83*

See pages 24–25 for pattern abbreviations.

SHOULDER BAG

Using colour A and 4mm Tunisian crochet hook, ch 45.

Row 1: Skip 1 ch, (insert hook in next ch, yrh, draw loop through ch only and keep on hook) repeat to end. Do not turn.

Row 2 (and all even rows): Yrh, draw through 1 loop, *yrh, draw through 2 loops, repeat from * until 1 loop remains on hook. Do not turn.

Row 3 (and all odd rows): Count loop on hook as first st and start in second st. *Insert hook at front and from right to left around single front vertical thread, yrh, draw through and keep on hook, repeat from * across. Do not turn.
Work a total of 98 rows. Break off yarn

GUSSET AND STRAP

Along one side of work, count in 45 rows from each end. Loop the centre 8 sts onto hook then starting with Row 2 of Tunisian simple stitch, work until you have completed 255 rows. Join with sl sts to the central 8 rows on the opposite side.

EMBROIDERY

Using the chart as a guide, stitch the design at the centre of the back and front of the bag. Use colours B and C, as indicated on the chart, threaded into a tapestry needle. Each square on the grid corresponds to one crochet stitch. Each cross stitch (see below) is worked over four crochet stitches (two rows of two stitches). This is also the size of the gap between each cross stitch.

JOINING AND EDGING

Using colour B, work two rows of dc on the two top edges of the bag. Then, starting at one of the lower corners of the bag and matching row for row, join the edge of the strap (which will form the gusset) to the edge of the bag, with a row of dc. When you reach the top of the bag, carry on in dc along the edge of the strap until you come to the opposite top edge, then continue as before, joining the edge of the strap to the edge of the bag. Repeat for the other side of the bag.

JOINING TIPS

The edge formed by this pattern is very firm and it is easy to match the ends of rows when joining. You may find it easier to pin the edge of the strap to the edge of the bag before you start to join them with a row of double crochet. Just remove each pin as you get to it.

CROSS STITCH

To make a cross stitch, bring the needle out at the top left of the four stitches you are going to cover. Insert it again at bottom right. Bring the needle out again at bottom left and insert again at top right to finish the stitch. Repeat, following the chart as a guide and changing colour as indicated.

EDGINGS

Many crocheted items benefit from a special edge or border. They not only

add interest, but give a better finish and help the crochet lie flat.

If an edging or border is to be the foundation for your main piece, make it first. If you are going to attach an edging afterward, make it separately. When working an edging, use a smaller size hook than you used for the main piece. This will give the edging a firmer finish.

To make an edging, normally you work one stitch into each stitch across the top of a row and into the underside of a foundation chain. When you get to a corner, you work three stitches into the corner and along the side of the fabric at the rate of one stitch per double crochet row. As a guide, you will need to use one and two stitches alternately per half treble crochet row, two stitches per treble crochet row, three stitches per double treble row, etc.

MAKING A CORDED EDGE

*Working from left to right, insert the hook into the next stitch to the right, yrh. Draw the loop through the work, below the loop which remains on the hook, and up to the left, into the normal working position (left). Yrh and draw the loop through to complete 1 corded double crochet (right). Repeat from *.*

DOUBLE-CROCHET EDGING

This basic edging, worked with the right side facing, neatens and strengthens the fabric and can cover any float yarns or stray short ends. It is also a good foundation for a more decorative edging.

BUTTONHOLE LOOPS

Loops for buttons may be made in an edging row by skipping the required number of stitches and working chains instead. If you need extra edging rows, work dc into the loops.

CORDED EDGE

This is a very effective edging, usually worked after one round of dc and with the right side facing. Work it in dc, but from left to right. (See below left.)

PICOT EDGING

Picots of varying size and complexity are a regular feature of crochet edgings. To make a simple picot, see page 73. For more complex designs, see page 87.

PICOT ARCHWAY

Multiple of 8 sts plus 1, plus 1 for foundation ch.

Row 1 (right side): Skip 2 ch, dc across, turn.

Row 2: Ch 1, dc across, turn.

Row 3: Ch 1 (does not count as dc), 1 dc, *ch 3, 2 tr in next, skip 2, 1 dc; rep from * across, turn.

Row 4: Ch 4 (counts as 1 tr, ch 1), 1 tr in first, * 1 dc in ch-3 loop, ch 6, 1 dc in ch-3 loop, (1 tr, ch 3, 1 tr – called V st) in dc; rep from * omitting 2 of 3 ch in last V st, turn.

Row 5: Ch 1, 1 dc in ch-1 sp, *[5 tr, ch 5, sl st in 5th ch from hook, 5 tr] in ch-6 loop, 1 dc in next ch loop; rep from * across.

BULLION SPIRALS

Foundation: Ch 12.

Special abbreviation bst (bullion stitch): Made with (yrh) 10 times (see page 67).

Row 1 (right side): Skip 3 ch, 1 tr, skip 3 ch, (1 tr, [1 bst, 1 tr] 3 times – called shell) in next, skip 3 ch, (3 tr, ch 2, 3 tr – called V st) in next, turn.

Row 2: Ch 7, skip 3 ch, [3 tr in next] 4 times, V st in ch-2 sp, ch 3, 1 dc in centre bst of shell, ch 3, 1 tr in each of last 2 sts, turn.

Row 3: Ch 3, 1 tr, skip 3 ch, shell in dc, skip 3 ch, V st in ch-2 sp, turn.

Rows 2 and 3 form the pattern.

PICOT SCALLOPS

Multiple of 8 sts plus 1, plus 2 for foundation ch.

Row 1 (right side): Skip 3 ch, 1 tr, *ch 1, skip 1, 1 tr; rep from * to last ch, 1 tr, turn.

Row 2: Ch 5 (counts as 1 tr, ch 2), tr2tog in first, *skip [1 tr, 1 ch], 3 tr, skip [1 ch, 1 tr], [tr2tog, ch 4, tr2tog – called 2cl] in ch sp; rep from * across, omitting last 2 ch and tr2tog from last 2cl and working 1 tr in same loop, turn.

Row 3: Ch 3 (counts as 1 htr, ch 1), 1 dc in ch-2 sp, *skip cl, [ch 3, 1 dc – called pc], skip 1, 1 pc, 2 pc in ch-4 loop; rep from * across, omiting 2nd pc at end of last rep and working ch 1, 1 htr in same loop, turn.

Row 4: Ch 1 (does not count as dc), 1 dc, *ch 1, skip 1 pc, [tr2tog, (ch 3, tr2tog) twice] in next pc, ch 1, skip 1 pc, 1 dc in next pc; rep from * across, turn.

Row 5: Ch 1 (does not count as dc), 1 dc, skip 1 ch, *[2 pc in next ch-3 loop] twice, skip 1 ch, 1 pc in dc; rep from * across.

TRIPLE PICOT

Multiple of 5 sts.

Note: All rows worked right side facing.

Row 1: With yarn matching main fabric, dc.

Row 2: With contrasting colour, *5 dc, [ch 3, sl st in 3rd ch from hook] 3 times, sl st in top of last dc made; rep from *.

(Main fabric represented here by a row of tr.)

| # LACE TRIM

Transform a plain sweater you buy or knit into something special with the addition of a narrow velvet ribbon and a length of sumptuous hand-crocheted lace.

✤ **SIZE**
One size: 3cm (1¼in) wide and 140cm (56in) long (to fit a V-necked cardigan of average size)

✤ **MATERIALS**
Yarn 4-ply 100% cotton, 1 x 50g ball
Hook One 4mm crochet hook
Notions 143cm (57¼in) of narrow velvet ribbon, sewing needle and thread to match ribbon and crochet trim

✤ **TENSION**
27 dc = 10cm (4in) (first row)
4 rows = 3cm (1¼in)

✤ **SKILLS USED**
Chain (ch), p11; double crochet (dc), p13; edgings, p86

See page 24–25 for pattern abbreviations.

LACE TRIM

Using 4-ply cotton and 4mm hook, ch 379; turn.

Row 1: Skip 2 ch, continue in dc to end of row.

Row 2: Ch 2, 1 dc *ch 3, skip 1, 3 dc, rep from * to last 3 sts; ch 3, skip 1, 2 dc; turn.

Row 3: Ch 2, *skip 1, (2 dc, ch 3, 2 dc) in ch-3 loop, skip 1, 1 dc, rep from * to end; turn.

Row 4: Ch 2, *(3 dc, ch 3, 3 dc) in ch-3 loop, 1 dc in dc of previous row, rep from * to end.

FINISHING

Stitch the narrow ribbon to the edge of the button band on the cardigan, turning each raw end under 1.5cm (⅝in). Pin the crochet trim in place. Pin the two ends to the two lower edges of the cardigan fronts, then pin the centre of the trim to the centre of the back neck edge. Then pin along the rest of the trim. Stitch in place.

SIZE GUIDE

The finished length of this lacy trim is 140cm (56in), made on a foundation chain of 379. If you want to make a longer or shorter length of trim, the foundation chain should be a multiple of 4 sts, plus 5, plus 2 for a turning chain.

If you find that it is slightly too long, ease in the extra as you pin it in place. This will give a slightly gathered appearance. If, however, you find that your finished work is too short, do not stretch it to fit as it will only shrink back to its original size when the garment is washed.

CORDS AND FINISHING TOUCHES

CORDS AND FINISHING TOUCHES

Crocheted buttons and cords will liven up accessories such as bags. Adding surface chains to a piece of finished crochet creates a decorative effect somewhat like weaving.

ALTERNATIVE IDEAS

You can use handmade cords for other handcrafted items – they are just as useful when teamed with knitted or sewn items. Use remnants of yarn to make cords for drawstring bags.

You might also want to experiment with alternatives to crochet cord. Ribbons, in varying thicknesses, can look very pretty threaded through crochet work. Or use purchased decorative cord, available in a range of contrasting colours.

You can use ordinary buttons on your crochet, but chunky crochet buttons are easy to make and offer a colourful, lively way of enhancing both knitted and crocheted garments and accessories. For a crochet buttonhole loop, see page 86.

Handmade cords are also useful – they can be used as ties and drawstrings to fasten openings in bags and garments. Both flat and round cords can be worked quickly and easily. Made in contrasting colours, they can add bright and decorative touches to crochet or knitted garments and accessories.

Surface chains are a way to apply additional pattern. Plaids need careful planning, but any crocheted design, particularly one with a network of chain spaces, may be decorated in this way with vertical or horizontal lines.

Made in the same dyed yarn as the bag, this rainbow-like cord is the perfect finishing touch (see page 58).

BOBBLE BUTTON

This is worked in the round. Make a foundation chain of 2 ch. Close this and each subsequent round with a sl st in first dc. Round 1 (right side): 6 dc in 2nd ch from hook. Round 2: Ch 1, 2 dc in each dc (12 sts). Round 3: Ch 1, 1 dc in each dc (left). Round 4: Ch 1, (1 dc, skip 1) 6 times (6 sts). Pack the button with a small amount of yarn (right). Round 5: Ch 1, (1 dc, skip 1) 3 times. Cut a length of yarn to close the opening and then sew the button in place.

ROUND CORD

Make a foundation ring: Ch 5 (or as required for thickness of cord). Work in a spiral around the ring as follows: 1 sl st in top loop of each ch and then of each sl st, until cord reaches required length. For a faster-growing cord, work in dc or tr.

FLAT CORD

Ch 2, 1 dc in 2nd ch from hook, turn and work 1 dc in ch at back of dc just made, *turn and work 1 dc, inserting hook down through 2 loops at back of dc just made; rep from * until cord is required length.

MAKING SURFACE CHAINS

1 Make a slip knot in new yarn. With right or wrong side facing as required, insert hook down through chosen chain space. Yrh underneath work, draw through work and loop on hook.

2 *Insert hook down through next chain space or selected position, yrh underneath fabric, draw through fabric and loop on hook; rep from * as required. Make one chain beyond edge of work and fasten off. It is important to work loosely so as not to distort the background stitches. It may help to use a larger hook than you used for the main work. Short ends of yarn should be worked over and encased during any subsequent edging rounds or darned into the wrong side of the piece.

FUNKY FLOWERS

Make a whole bunch of flowers, in different colourways, to make

the perfect finishing touch for lapels, hats, sweaters,

chokers and wristbands.

❖ SIZE

*One size: Flower is 7.5cm (3in) wide. Leaf is 6cm (2¼in)
long and 4cm (1½in) wide*

❖ MATERIALS

Yarn *Small amounts of cotton glacé in colour A (for
flower) and colour B (for leaves)*
Hook *One 2mm hook*
Notions *Tapestry needle, pearl button*

❖ TENSION

Each flower measures 7.5cm (3in) across

❖ SKILLS USED

*Chain (ch), p11; slip stitch (sl st), p11; double crochet
(dc), p13; treble crochet (tr), p15; double treble crochet
(dtr), p15; changing colours, p39; working in the round,
p53*

See page 24–25 for pattern abbreviations.

FUNKY FLOWERS

Each flower is made in two parts: An outer set of petals and a smaller centre.

OUTER PETALS

Using cotton glacé in colour A and 2mm hook, ch 9, join with a sl st in first ch to form foundation ring.

Round 1: Ch 3, 2 tr into ring, (ch 6, sl st sideways into top of last tr, 3 tr in ring) 5 times, ch 6, sl st sideways into top of last tr, sl st in 3rd ch of ch-3.

Round 2: Sl st into first tr of previous round, (11 tr into ch-6 loop, sl st in centre tr of 3 tr group) 5 times, 11 tr into ch-6 loop, sl st to first sl st. Fasten off.

TIPS AND HINTS

As with all small-scale crochet projects, this is an ideal way to use up scraps from larger projects. Use your own colour combinations: you could make the inner and outer parts of the flower from different colours. You could also try a fancy button for the middle of your flower.

CENTRE PETALS

Make a foundation ring of 9 ch, as before, and work round 1 only; fasten off.

LEAF

Using cotton glacé in colour B and 4mm hook, ch 10; turn.

Row 1: 1 sl st into each of first 3 ch, 1 dc into each of next 3 ch, 1 tr into each of next 3 ch, 5 dtr into last ch. Now work back down the other side of the foundation ch: 1 tr into each of next 3 ch, 1 dc into each of next 3 ch, 1 sl st into each of last 3 ch.

Row 2: 1 sl st into each of first 3 sts, 1 dc into each of next 3 sts, 1 tr into each of next 3 sts, 1 dtr into each of next 2 sts, 3 dtr into next st, 1 dtr into each of next 2 st, 1 tr into each of next 3 sts, 1 dc into each of next 3 sts, 1 sl st into each of last 3 sts. Fasten off. Make more leaves, as required.

FINISHING

Stitch the outer and centre petals together and stitch a button over the hole in the centre. Stitch a leaf or leaves to the back of the flower, attaching the pointed ends to the centre back of the flower.

DYEING YARNS

Although store-bought yarns come in a wide range of colours, you might want to try something a little different. Experiment with dyeing yarns and you can guarantee your finished crochet will be unique.

Start with white 100 per cent cotton yarn. Use cold water dyes and be careful to follow the manufacturer's instructions to ensure the dyed yarn remains colourfast – in other words, the colour will not run when you wash the finished garment. Wear rubber gloves when handling the dyes to protect your hands.

DYEING YARNS

Yarn is sometimes available in hanks. If, however, you are starting with a ball of yarn, you will need to unwind it and then rewind it into a loose hank. Tie the hank loosely with short lengths of yarn in two or three places.

Wash the hank of yarn in soapy water then rinse thoroughly in several changes of clean water. Wring out excess water and leave damp.

Dissolve the dye powder and mix with water, soda and salt, according to the manufacturer's instructions. Pour each colour into a separate bucket or deep bowl (top picture). For this yarn, three different colours have been used.

Immerse a portion of the hank into one of the buckets of dye. In the middle picture, about half the yarn is immersed in yellow dye. Place a wooden spoon or stick across the top of the bucket, to support the yarn and keep the undyed part out of the dye. You will need to leave the yarn immersed in the dye for about 1 hour.

Remove the yarn from the dye and squeeze out excess. Then immerse another portion of the hank in another colour – in the bottom picture, a quarter of the yarn is dipped in blue dye. Then repeat with a third colour until the desired result has been achieved.

Wash the dyed yarn in soapy water and rinse thoroughly, then leave to dry before winding into a ball. The dyed yarn is then ready to use.

Simple sash belt
Rowan Summer Tweed
Exotic #512

String bikini top
Rowan Cotton Glacé
Pier #809

Peek-a-boo cushion cover
Rowan Handknit Double Knitting
Cotton
Colour A Chime #204
Colour B Flame #254

Striped halter top
Rowan Lurex Shimmer
Colour A Minty #337
Colour B Bedazzled #338

Zigzag scarf
Debbie Bliss Merino Double
Knitting
Colour A #605
Colour B #607

Twenty-squares throw
Jaeger Matchmaker Merino Aran
Colour A Pink #773
Colour B Charcoal grey #639

Bucket hats
Adult hat:
Rowan Cotton Glacé
Sunny #802

Baby hat:
Rowan 4-ply Cotton
Cheeky #133

Multicoloured bag
12-gauge cotton yarn, dyed to
shade required

Beaded bag
Rowan 4-ply Cotton
Ripple #121

Tubular tote
Rowan Cotton Glacé
Colour A Sky #749
Colour B Splendour #810
Colour C Bleached #726

Pet basket with liner
Utility string

Granny square top
Rowan 4-ply Cotton
Colour A Zest #134
Colour B Cheeky #133
Colour C Fennel #135
Rowan Cotton Glacé
Colour D Splendour #810

Bobble hat
Rowan Yorkshire Tweed Double
Knitting
Revel #342

Lacy camisole
Rowan 4-ply Cotton
Orchid #120

Mesh cover-up
Rowan Denim
Memphis #229

Hardworking shoulder bag
Rowan Cotton Glacé
Colour A Zeal #813
Colour B Mystic #808
Colour C Shoot #814

Lace trim
Rowan 4-ply Cotton
Bluebell #136

Funky flowers
Rowan Cotton Glacé
Colour A Tickle #811
Colour B Shoot #814

ACKNOWLEDGMENTS
The author would like to thank Rowan Yarns for all their help in supplying yarns for this book.

Carroll and Brown would like to thank The Mayhew Animal Home (www.mayhewanimalhome.org) for their assistance with this project.

Production Karol Davies
IT Paul Stradling
Photographic Assistant David Yems

SUPPLIERS

Rowan/Jaeger (UK)
Green Lane Mill
Holmfirth
West Yorkshire HD9 2DX
Tel 01484 681881
www.knitrowan.com
mail@knitrowan.com